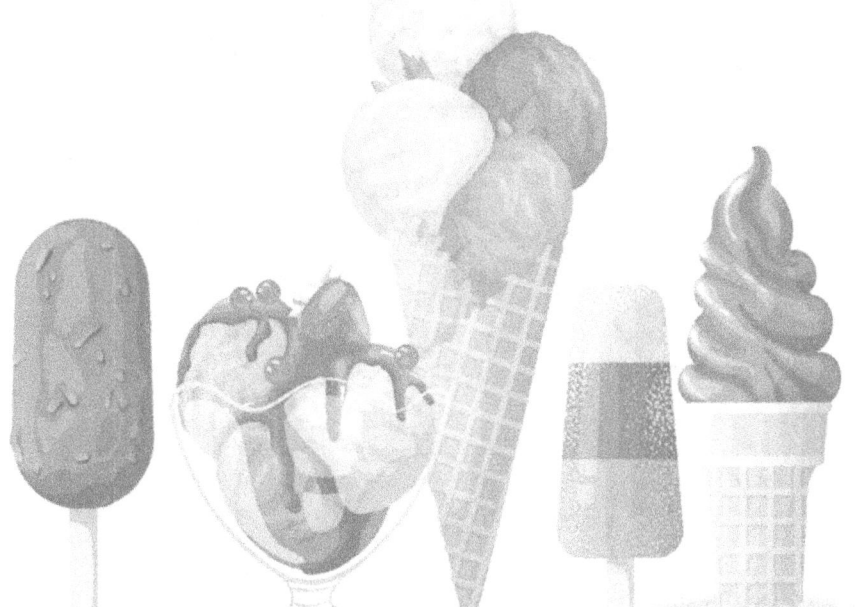

This Book Belongs To:

_____

_____

_____

_____

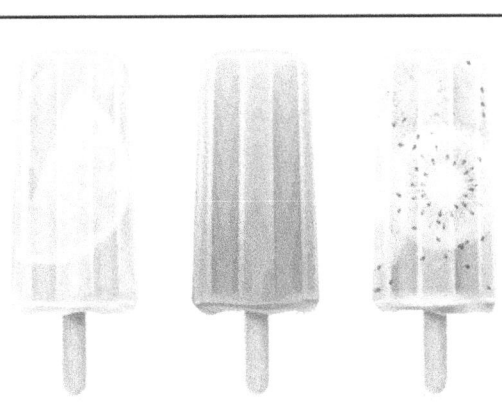

Test Your Color

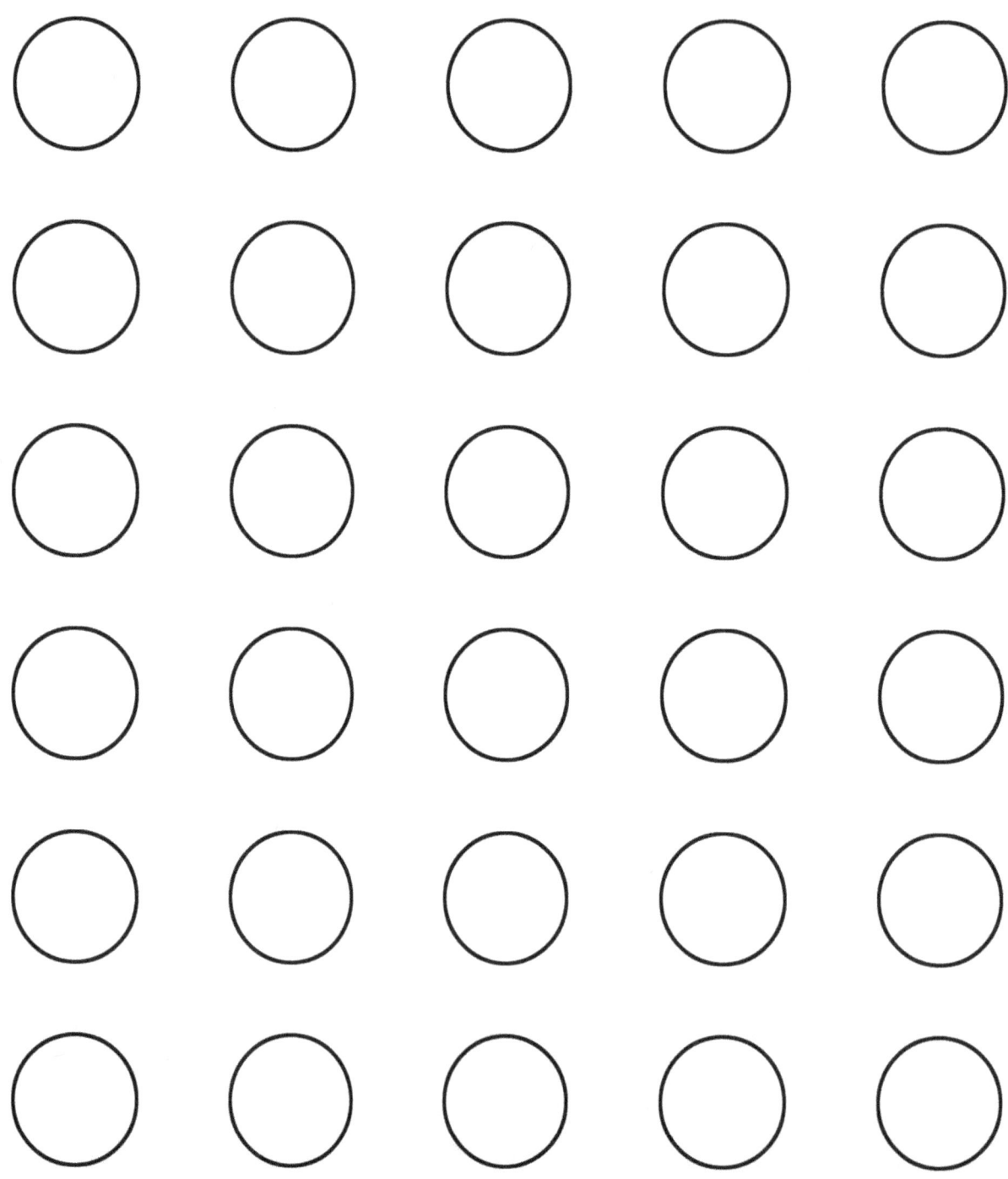

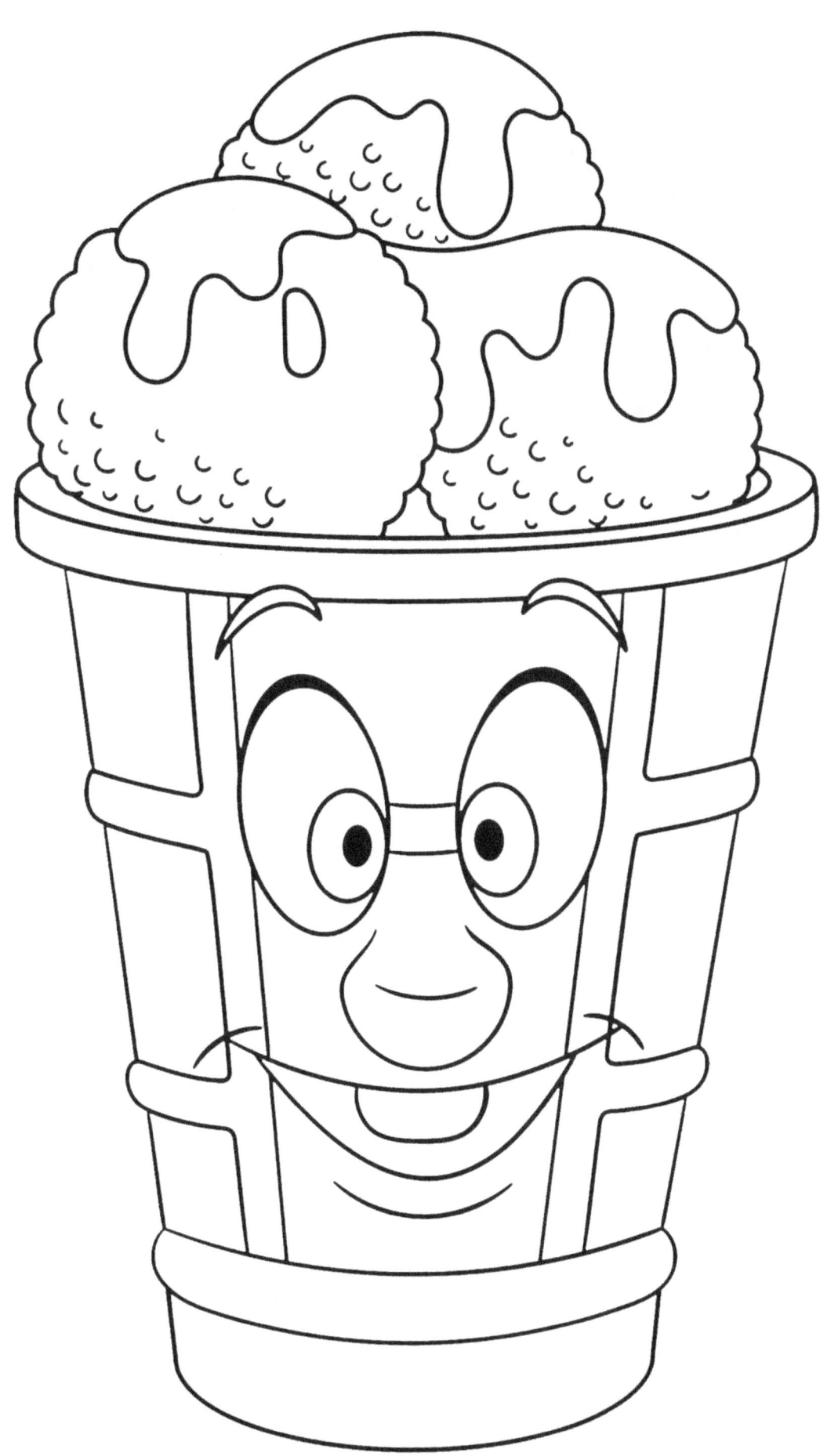

Test Your Color

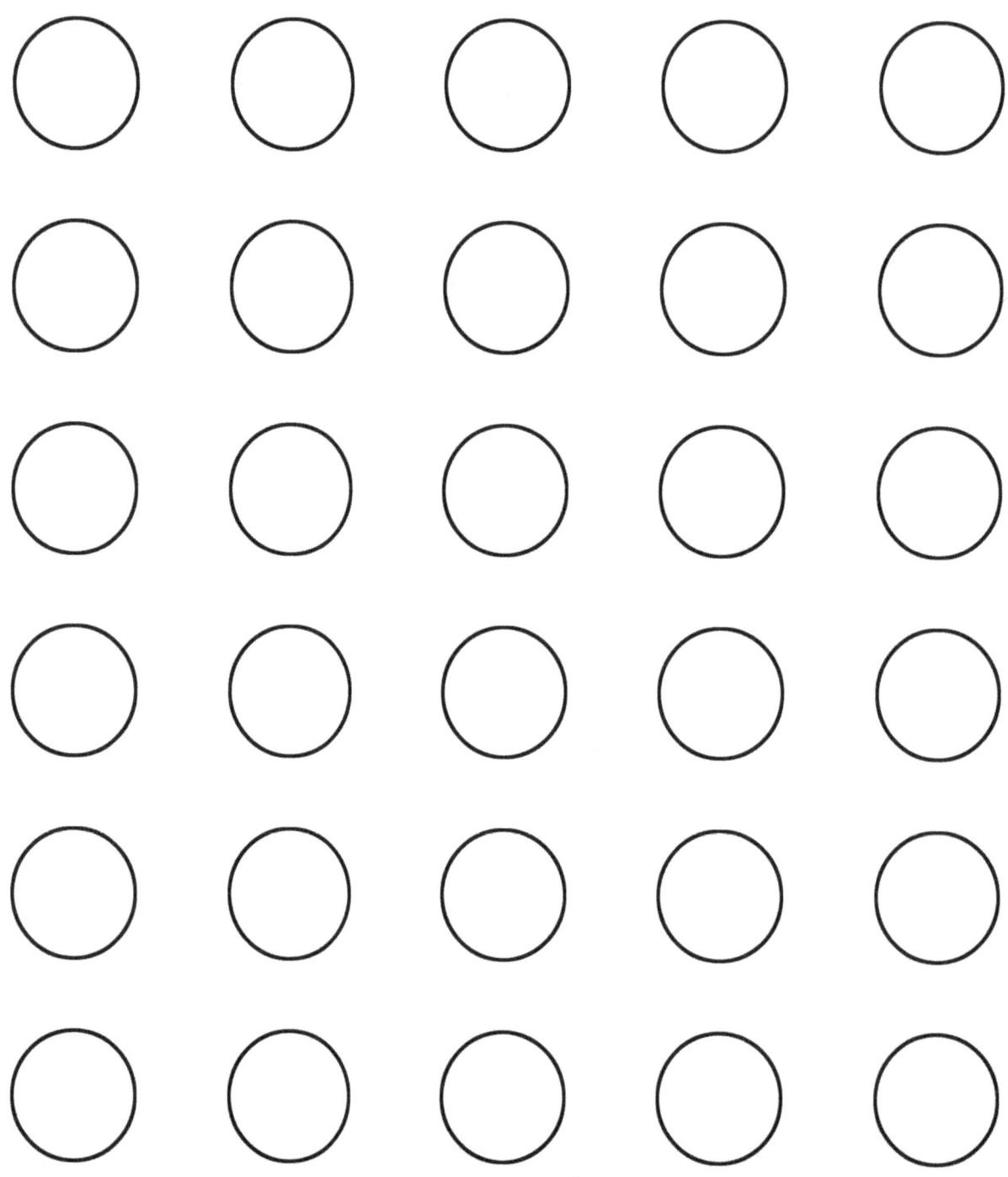

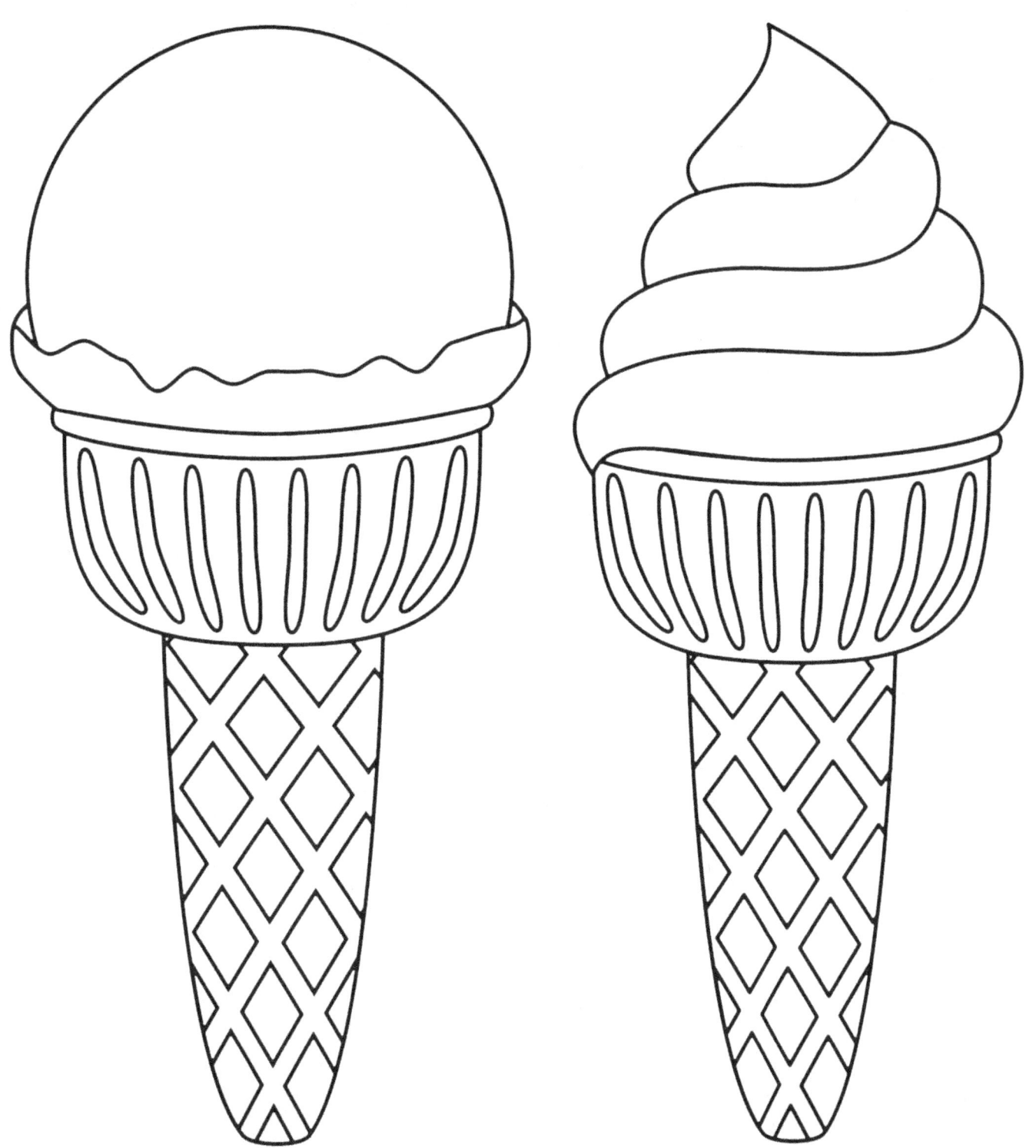

Test Your Color

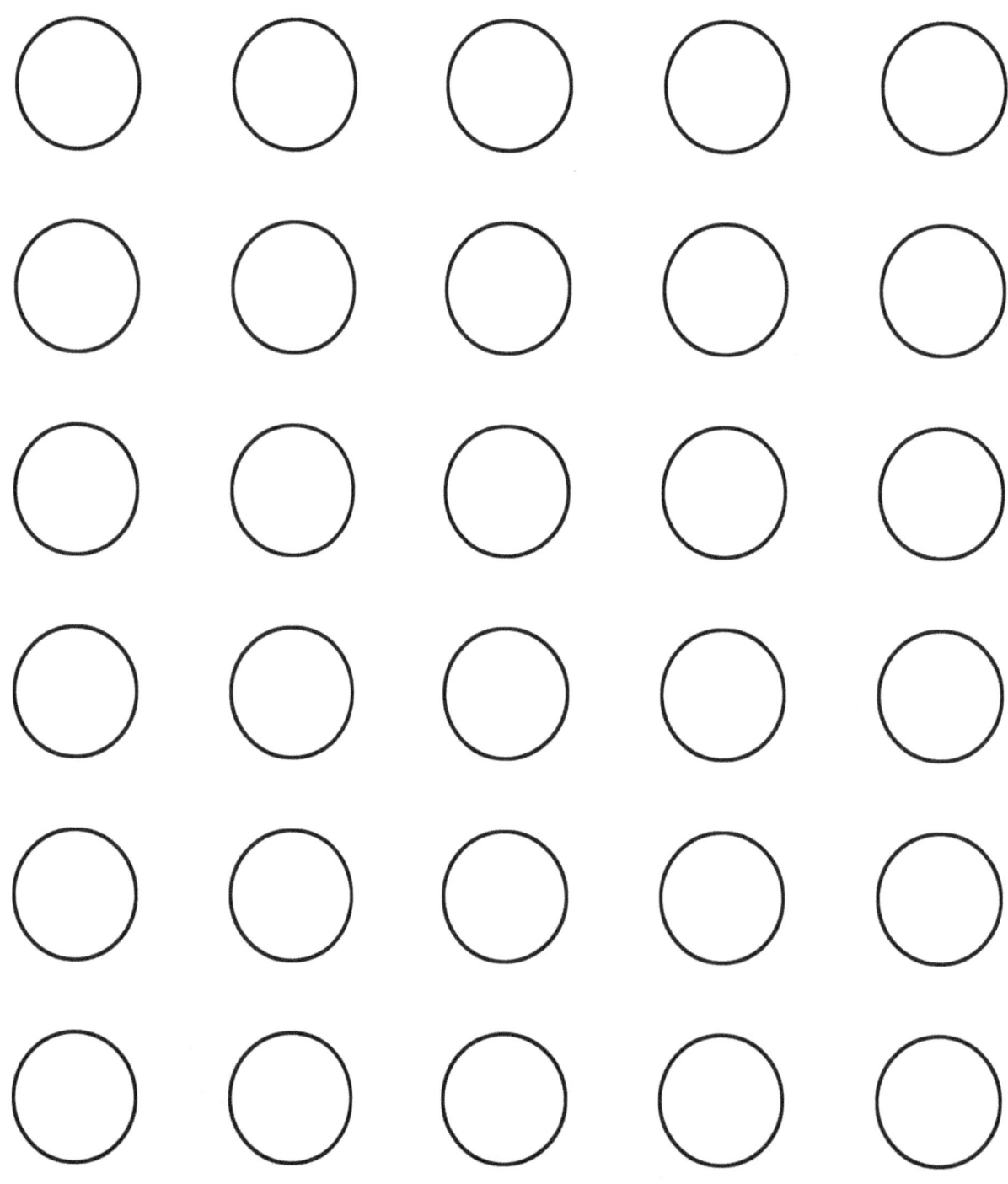

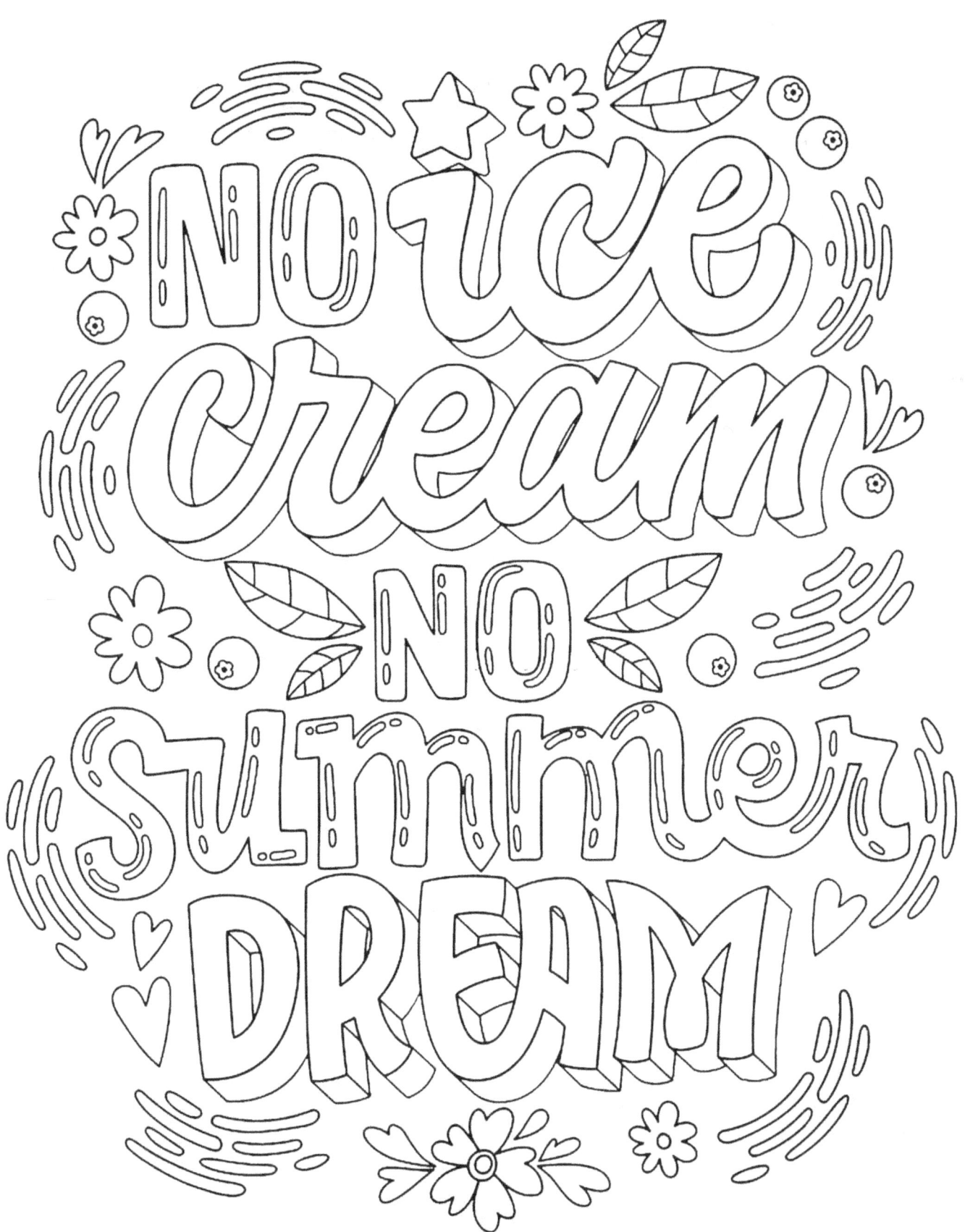

Test Your Color

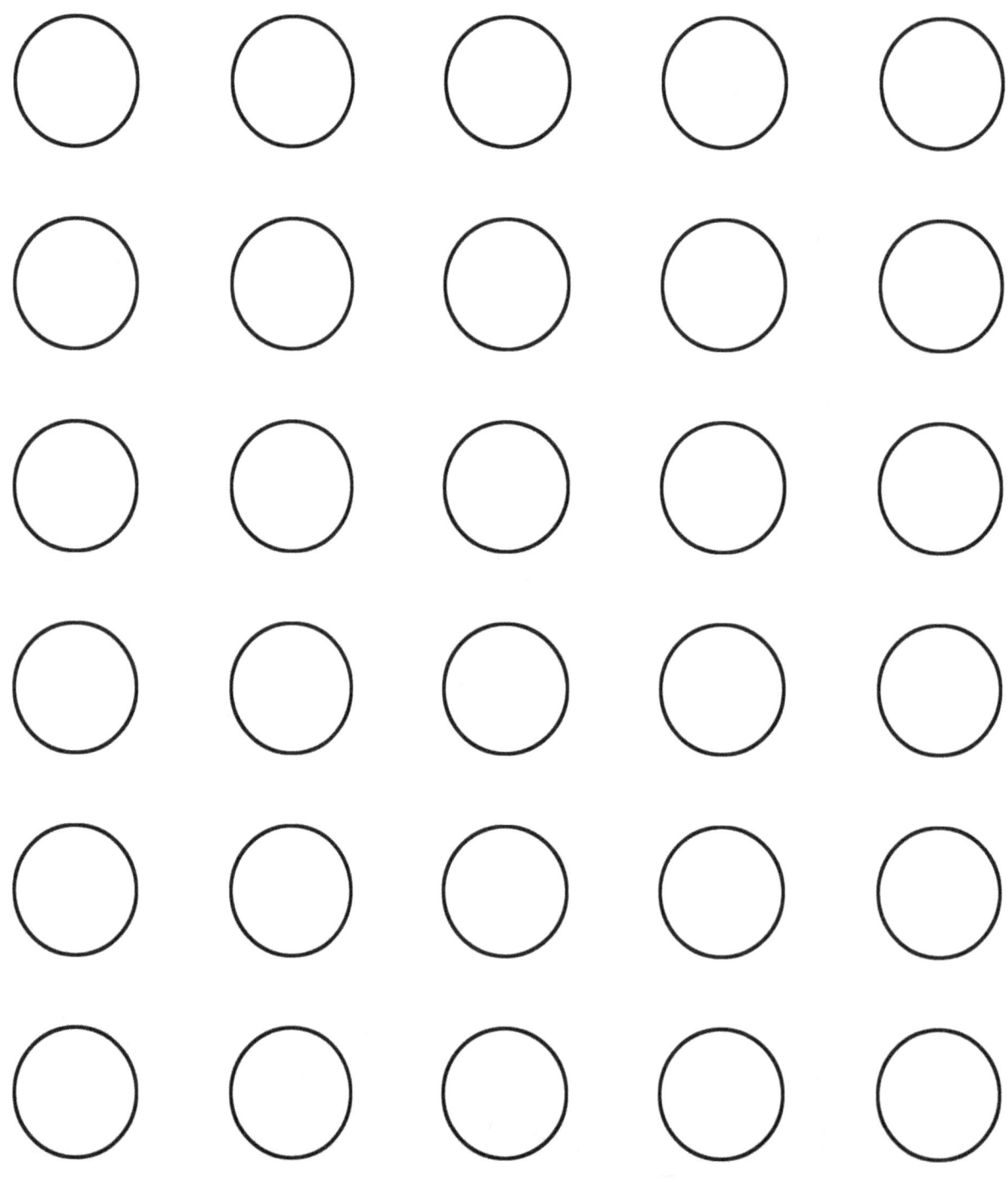

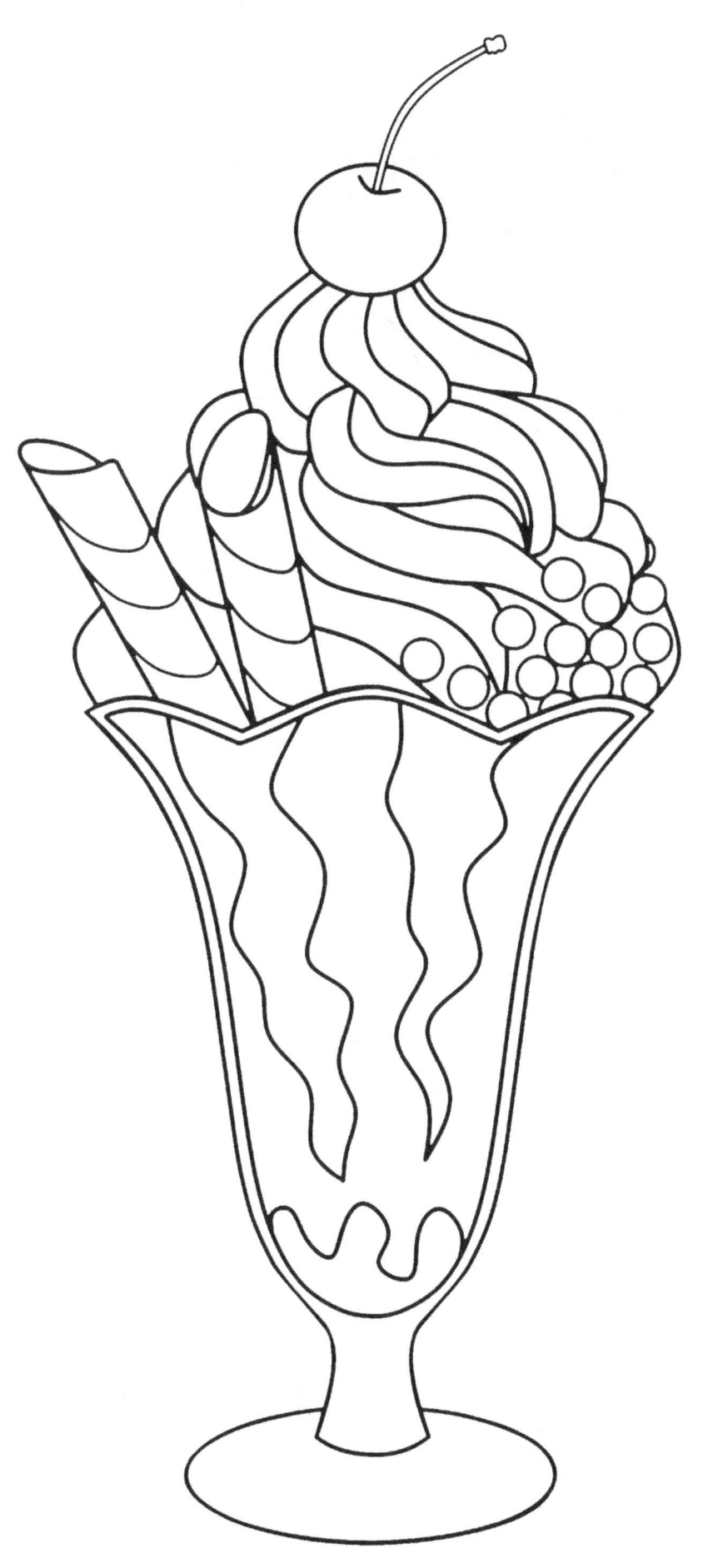

Test Your Color

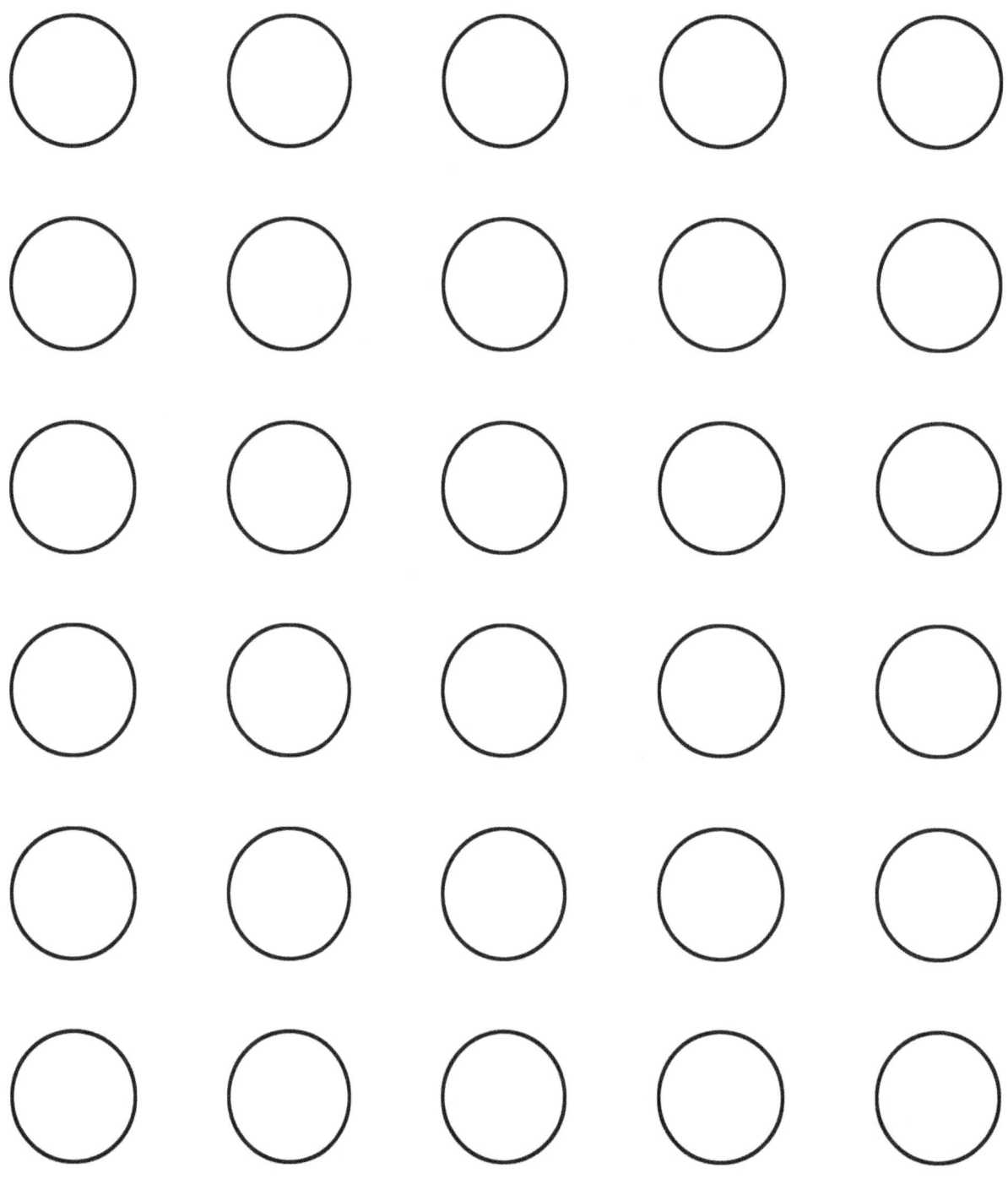

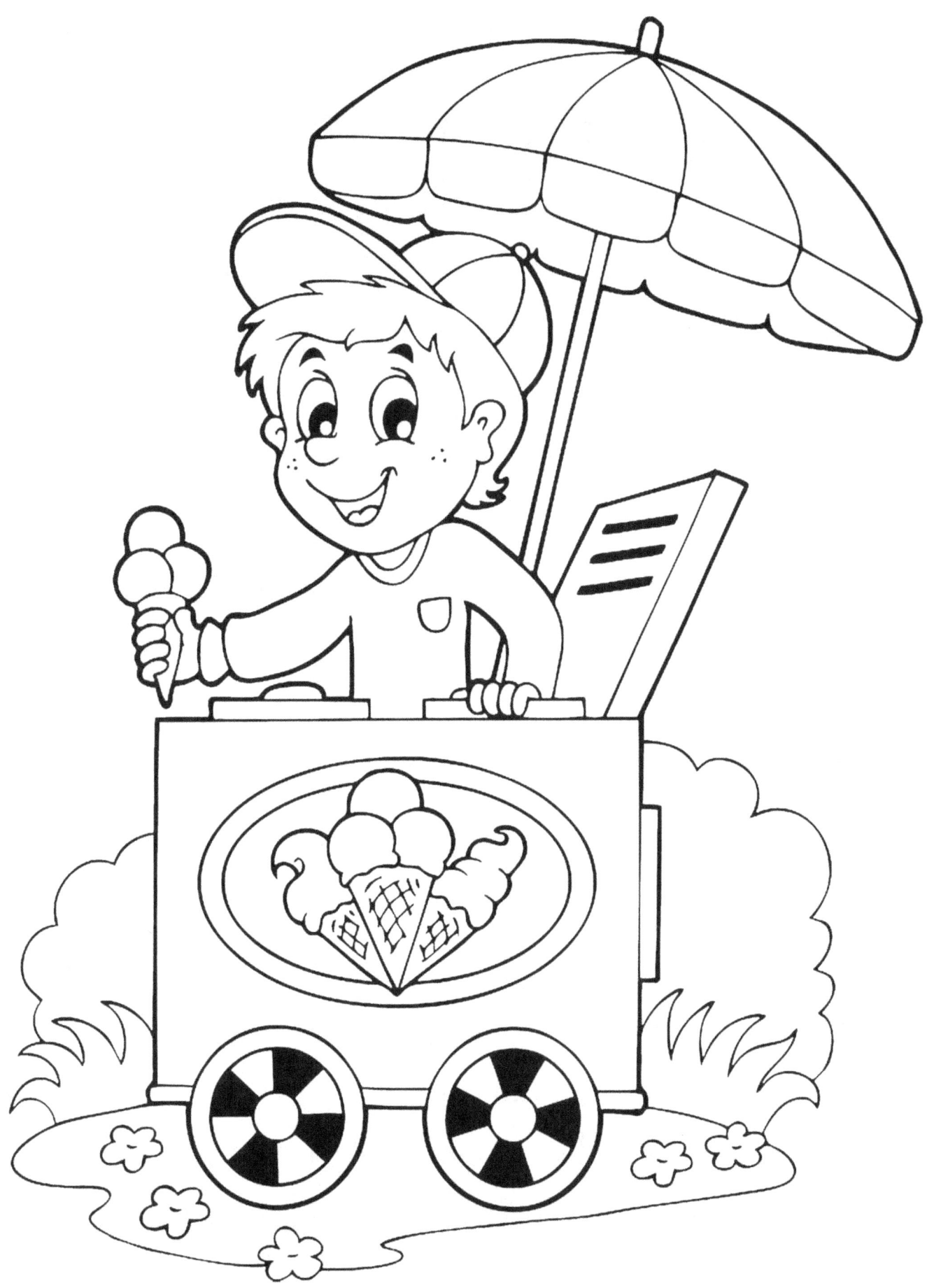

Test Your Color

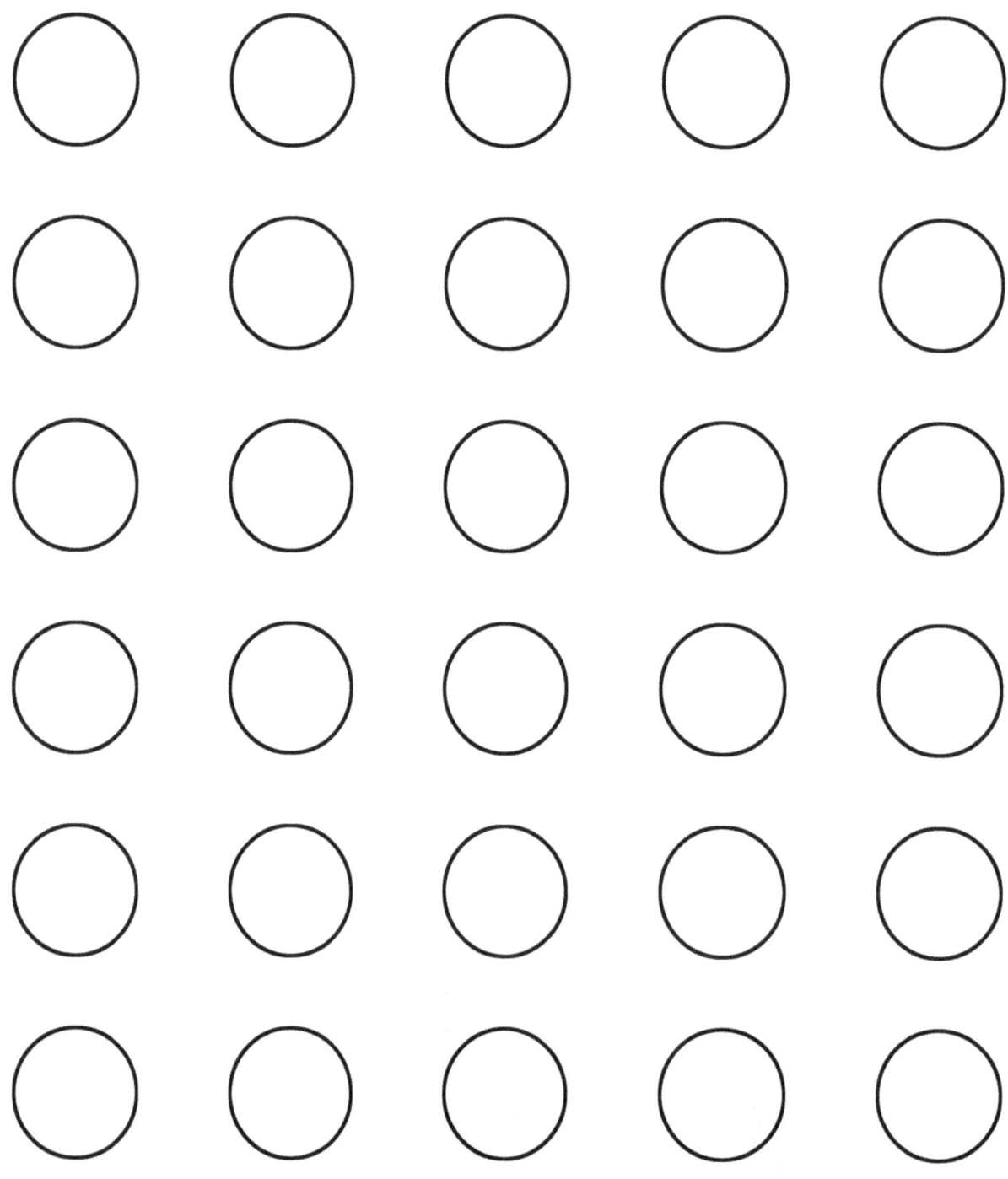

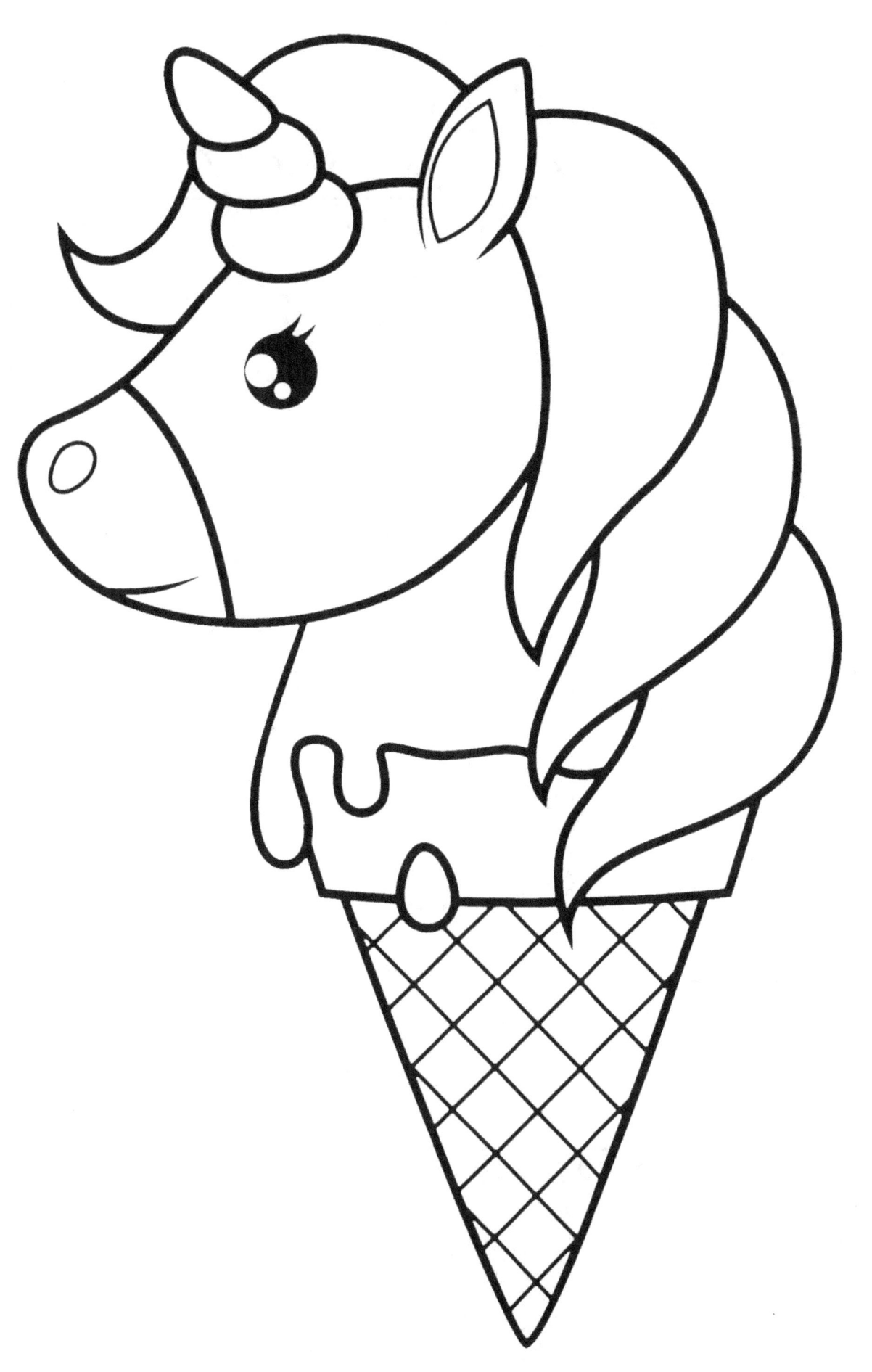

Test Your Color

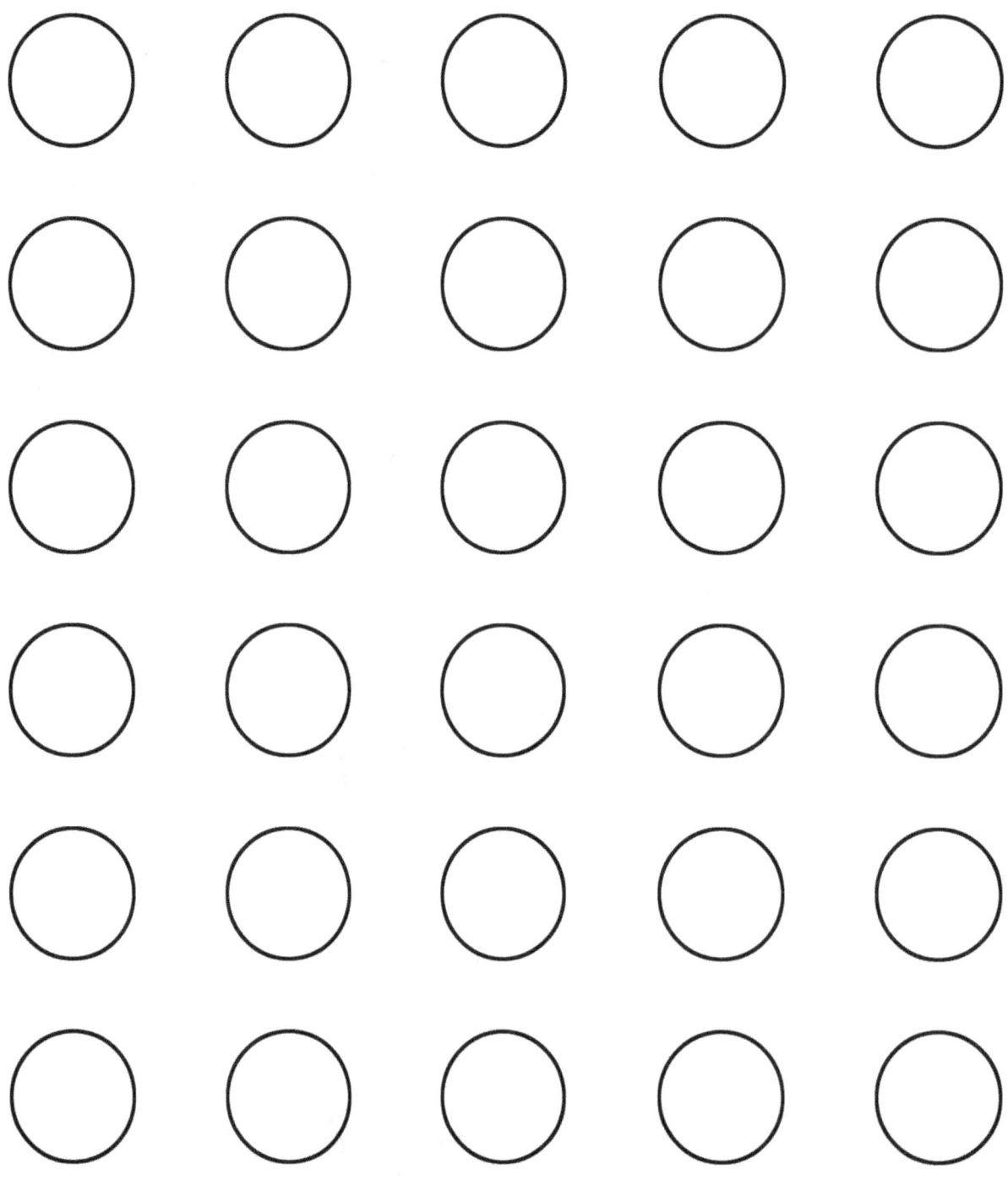

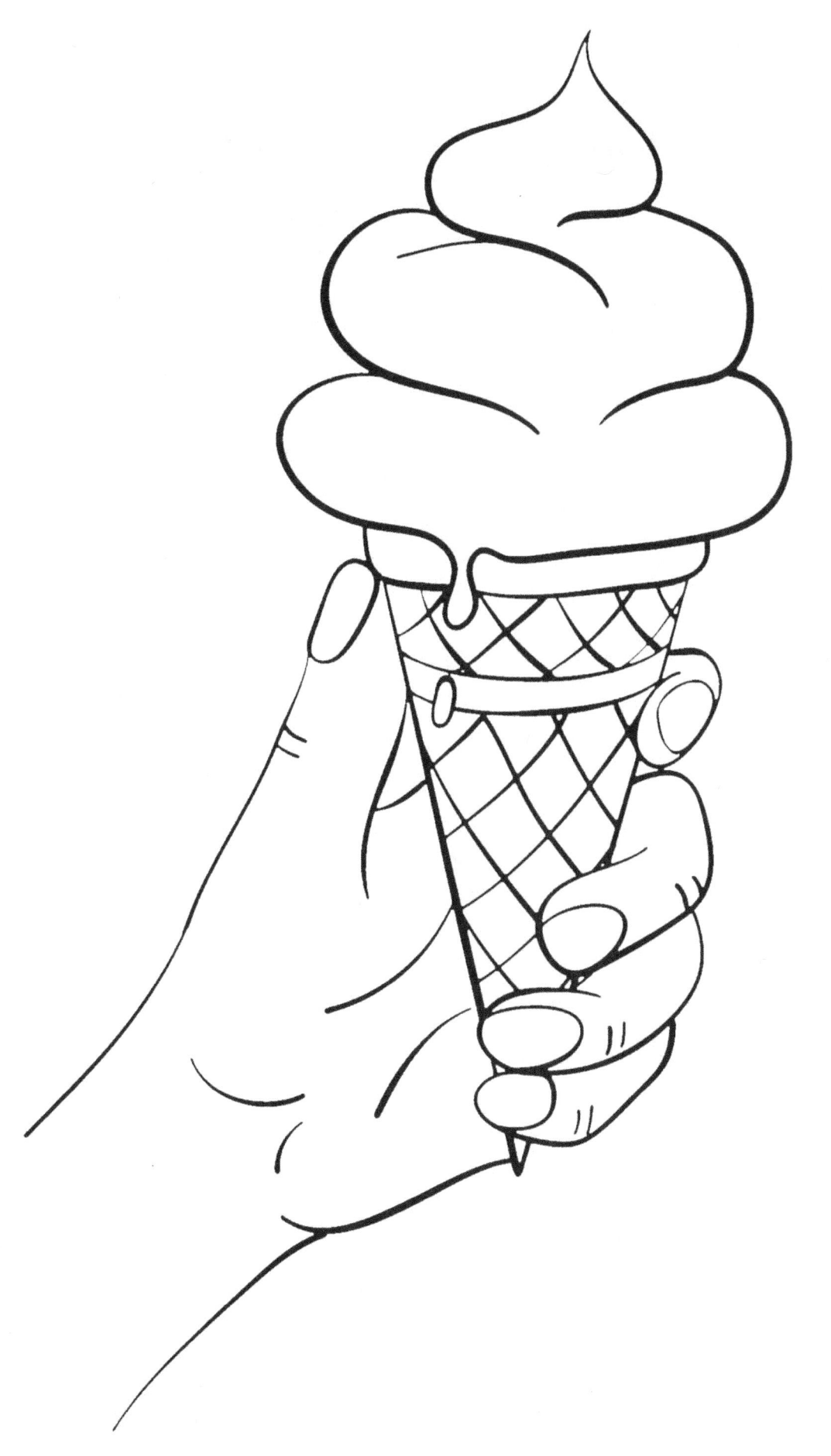

Test Your Color

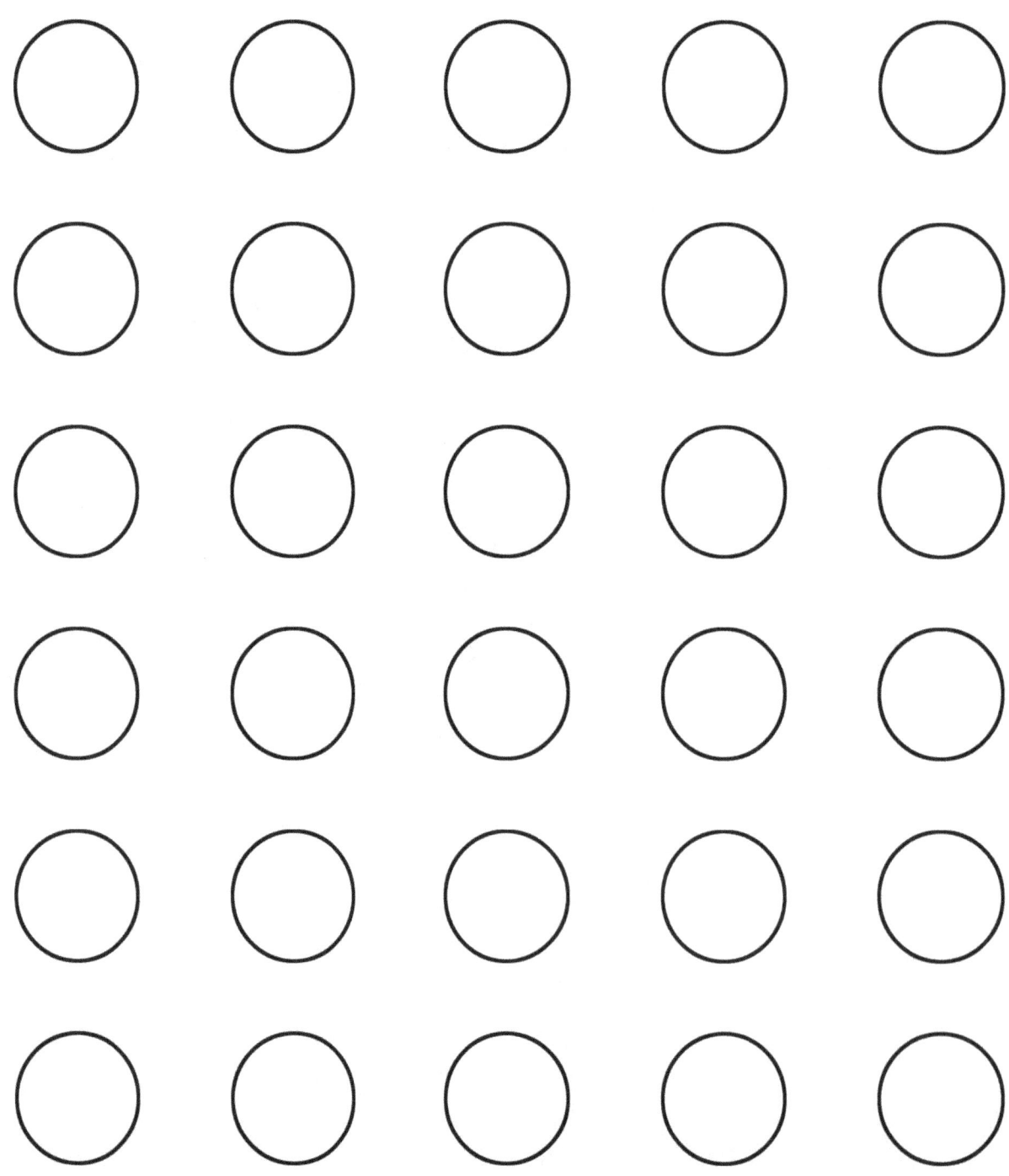

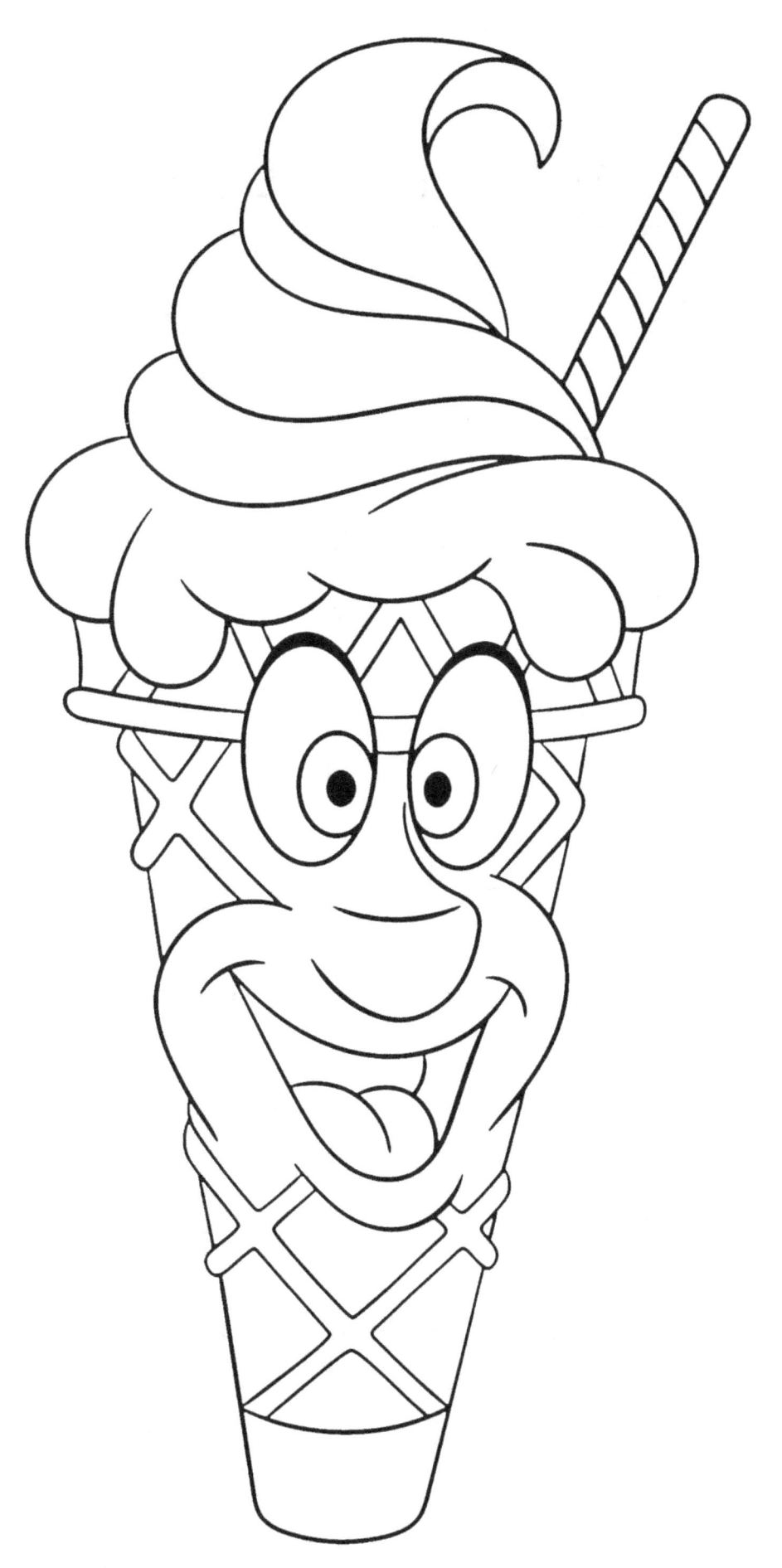

Test Your Color

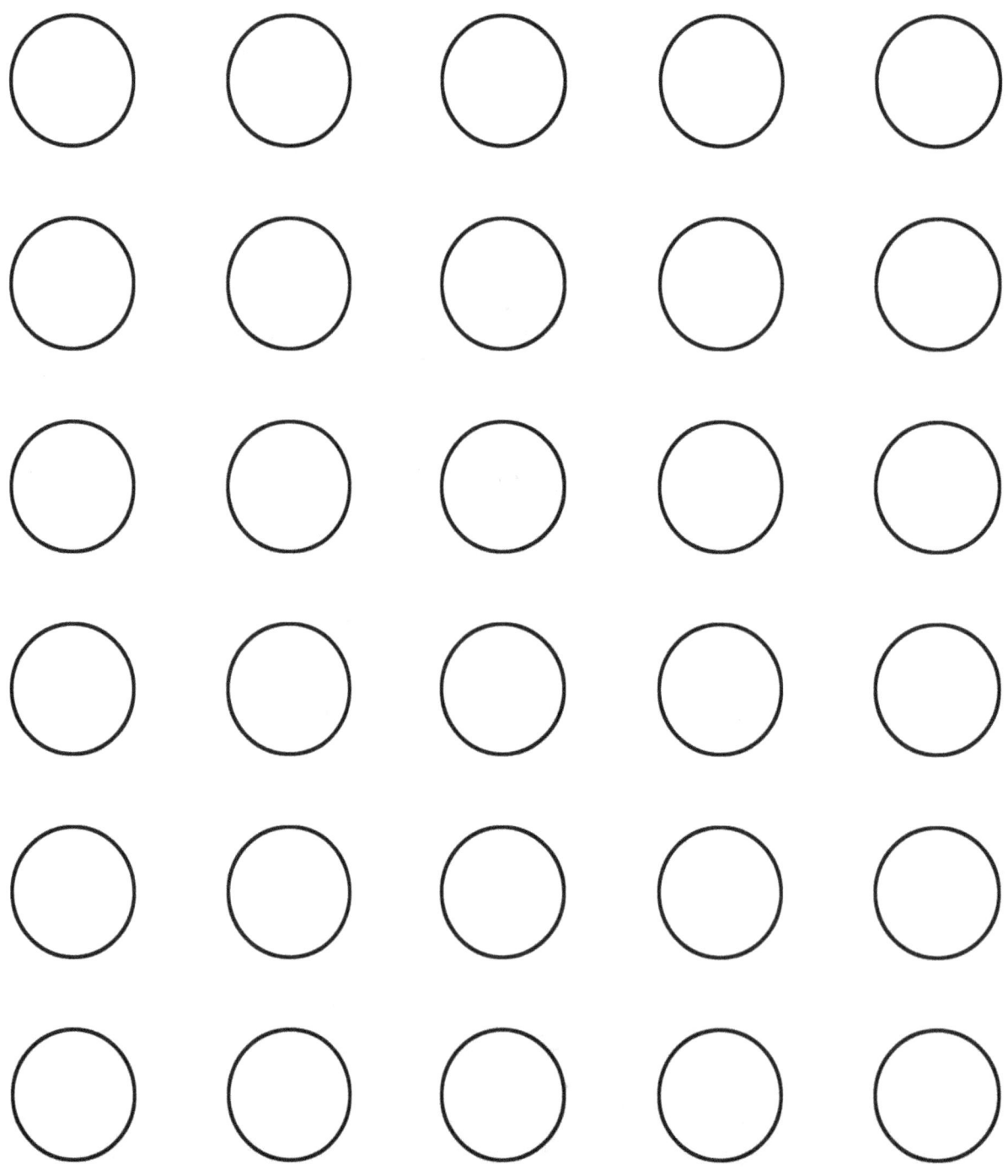

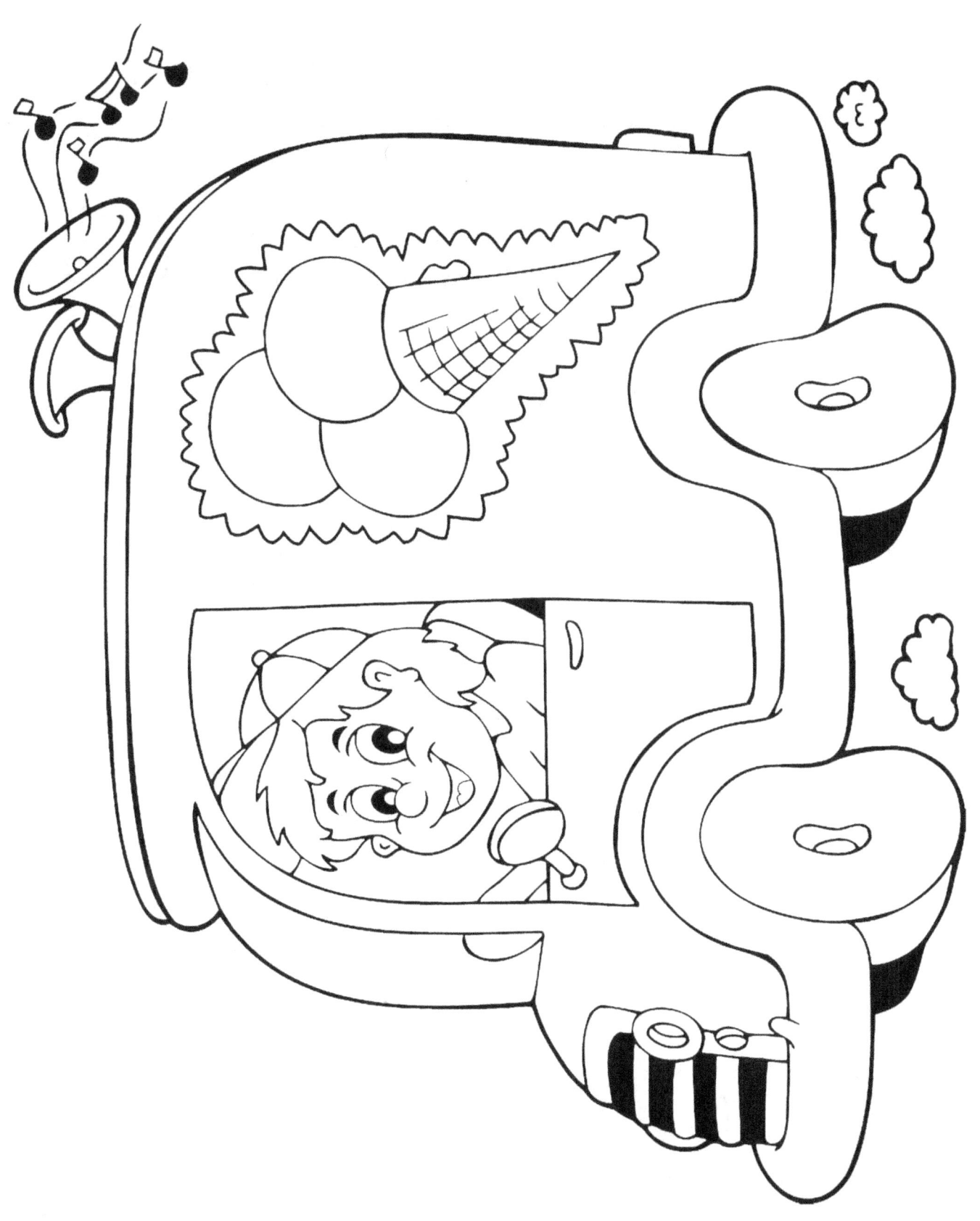

Test Your Color

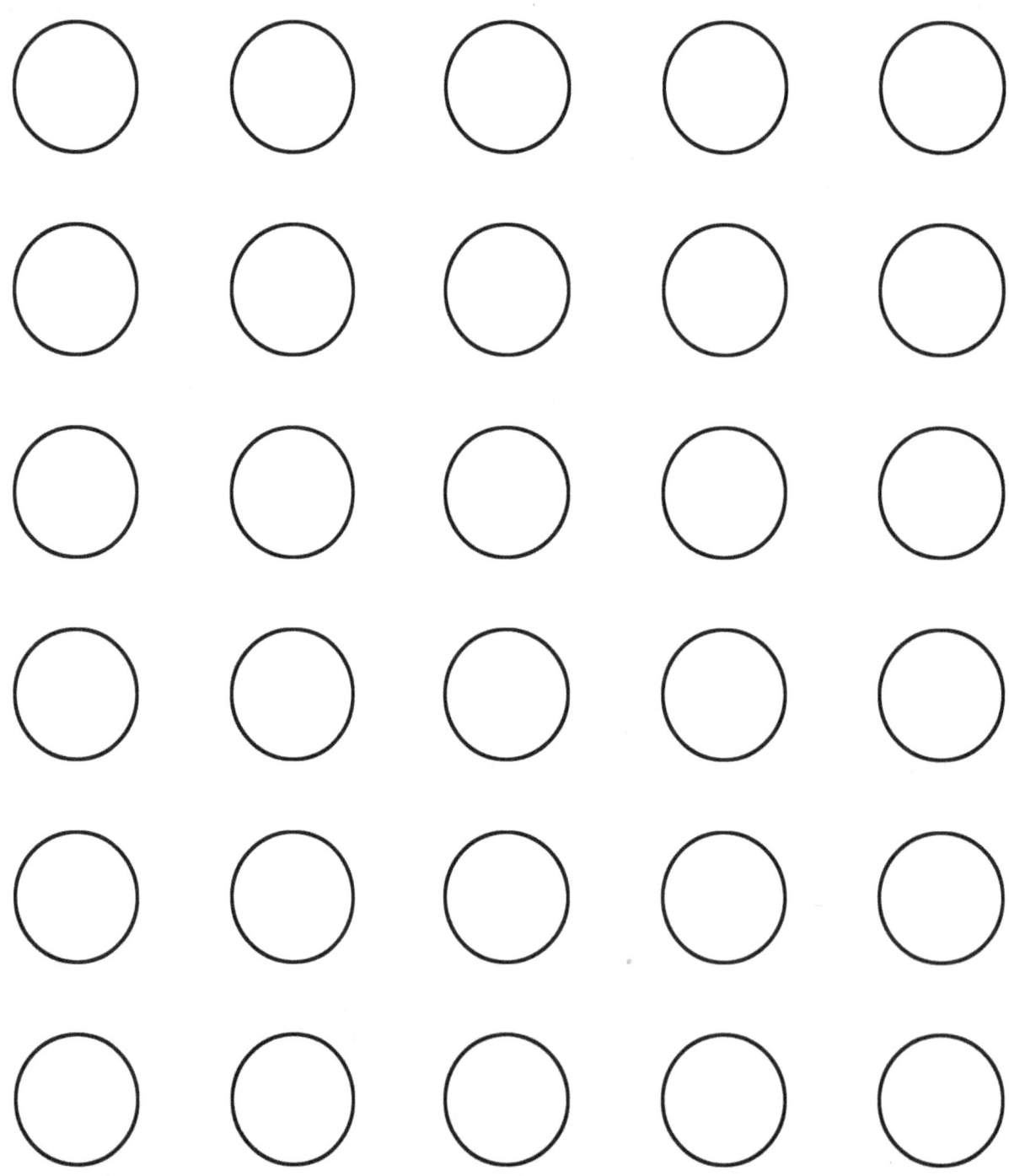

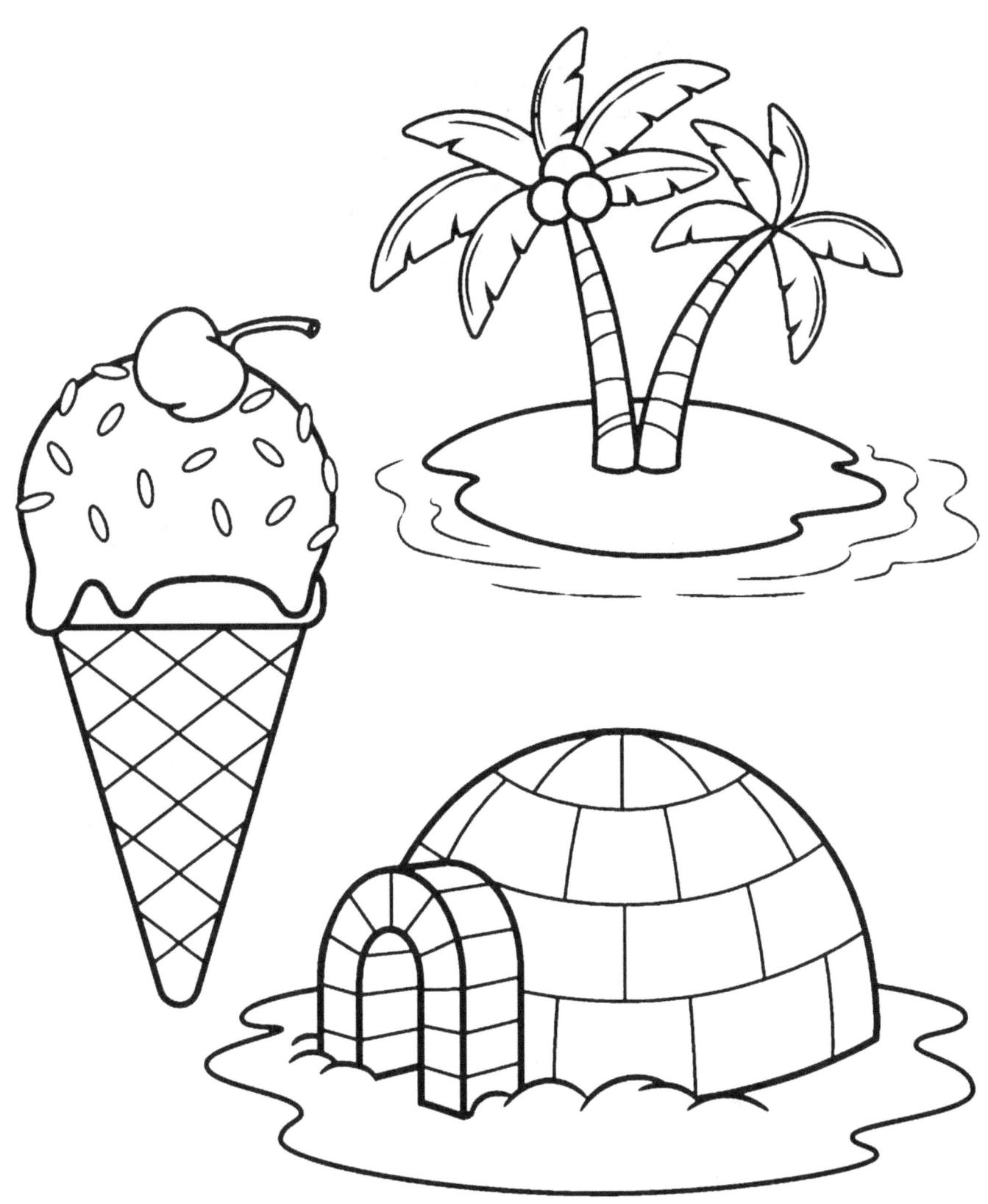

Test Your Color

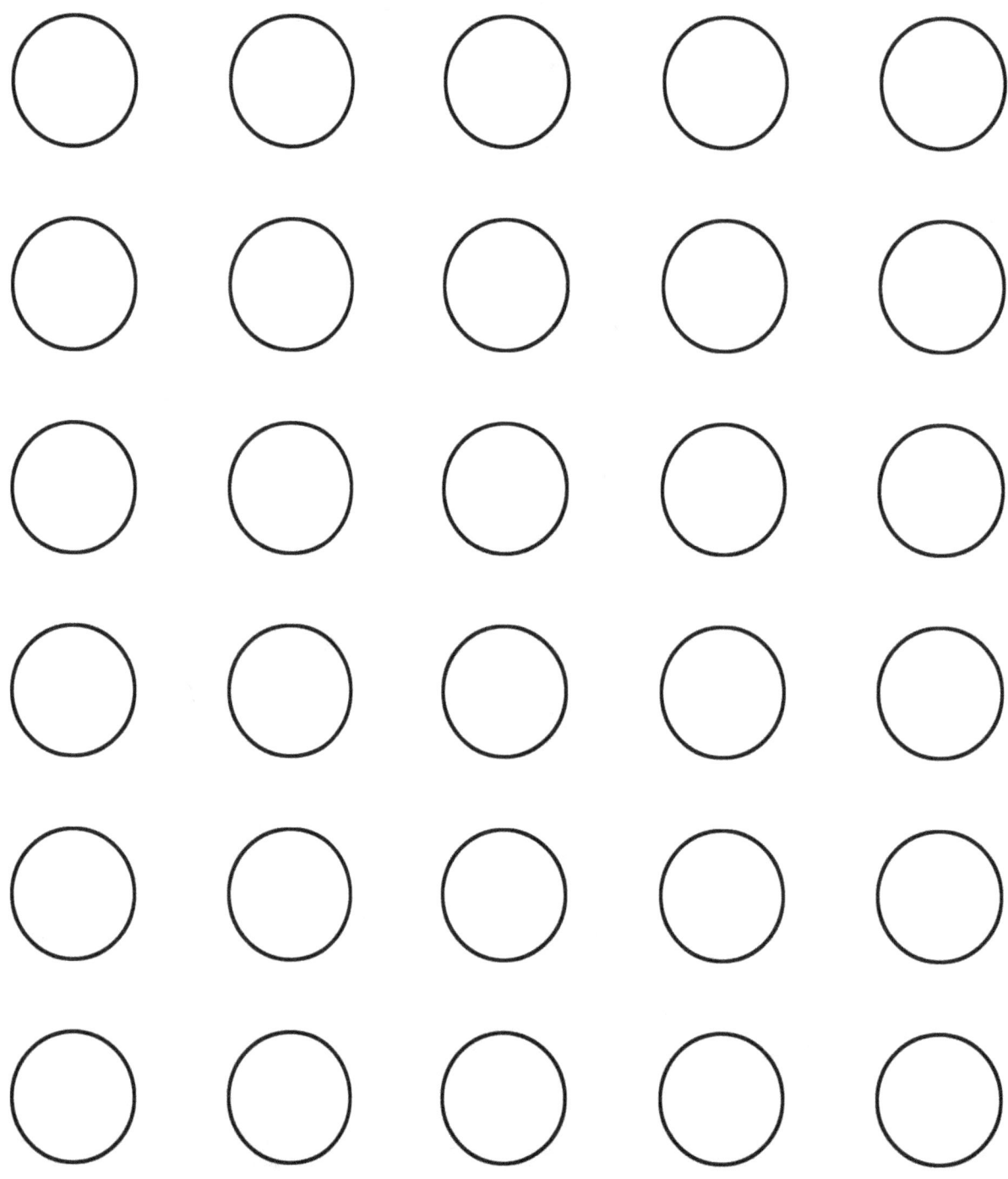

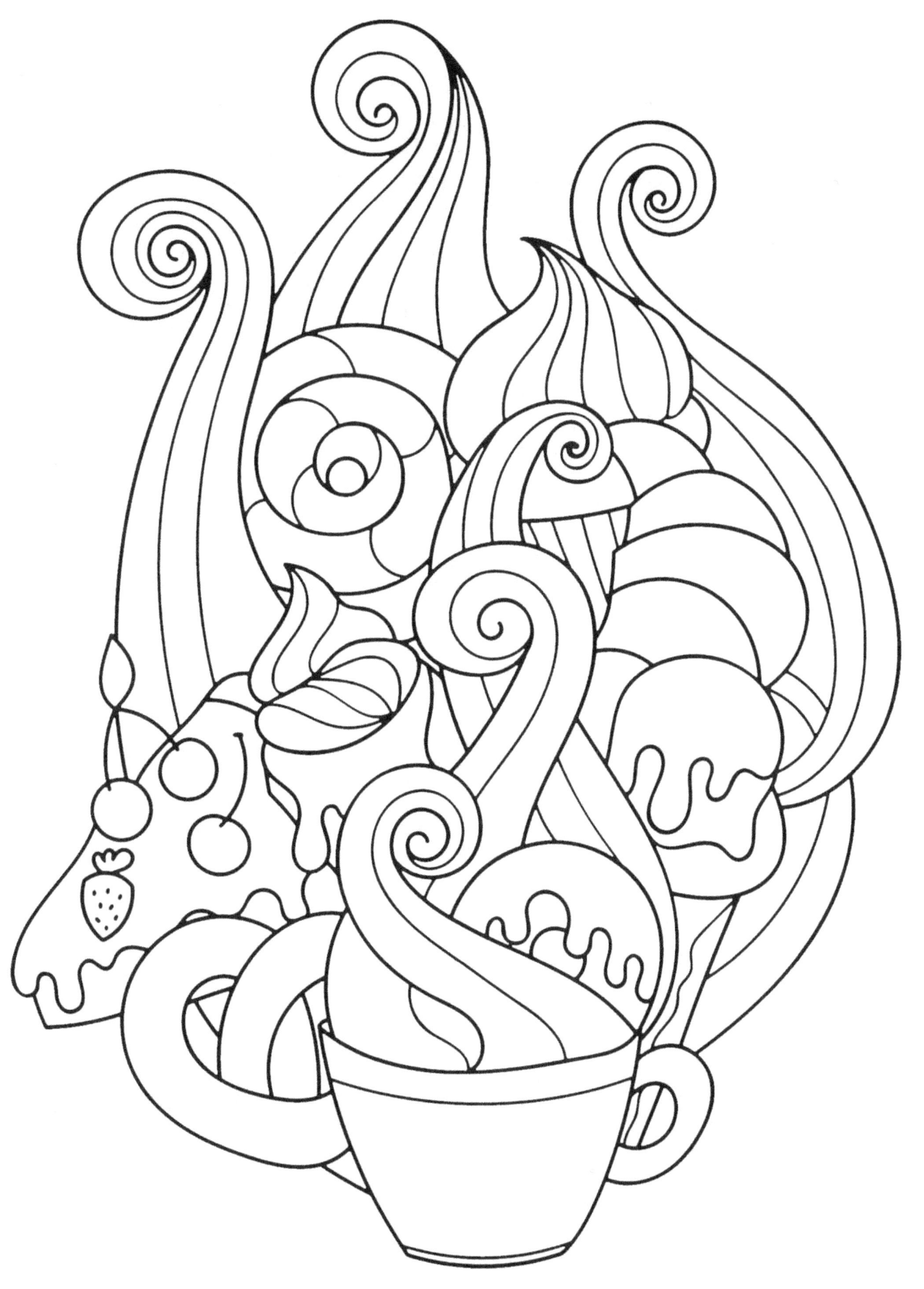

Test Your Color

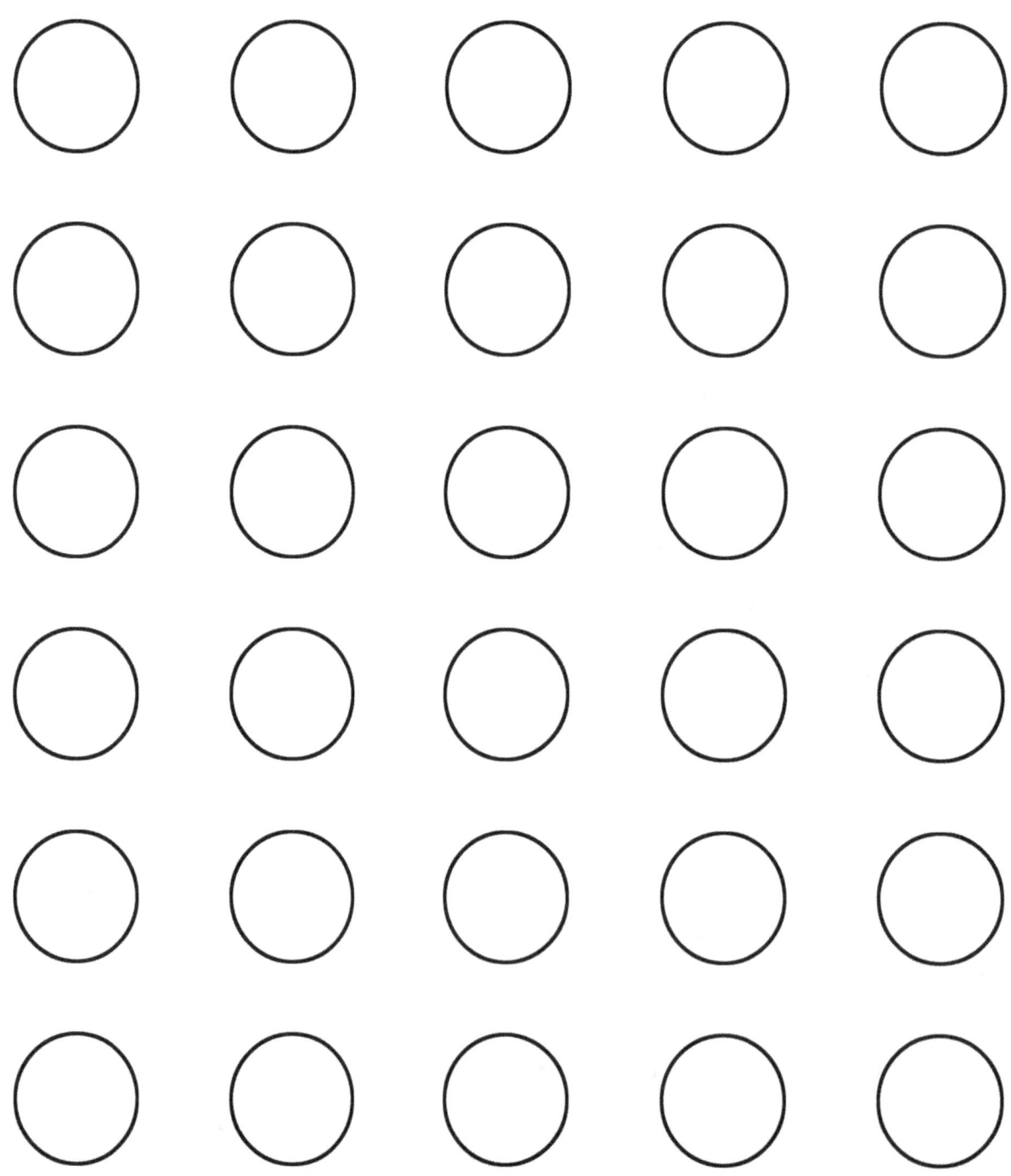

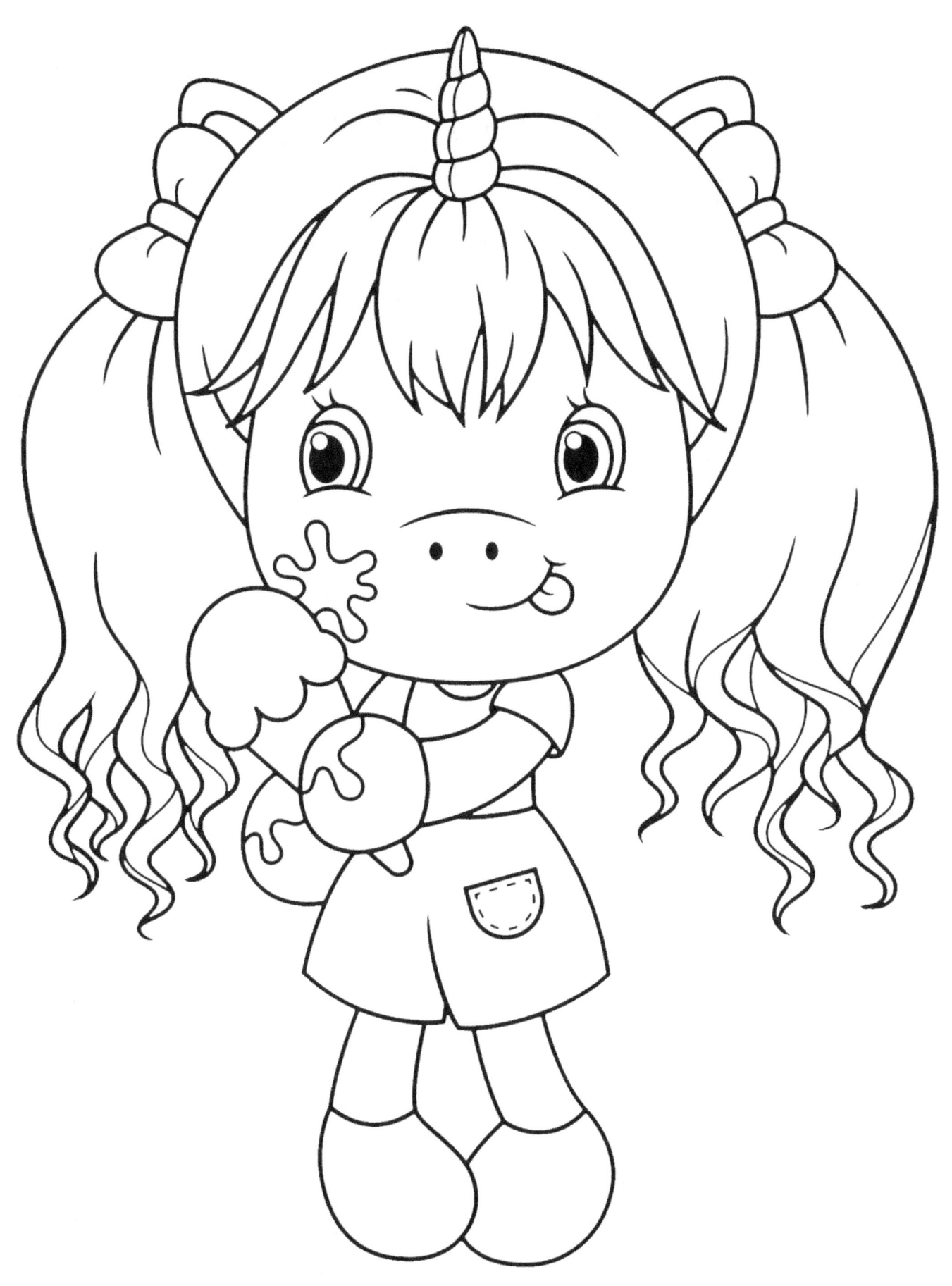

Test Your Color

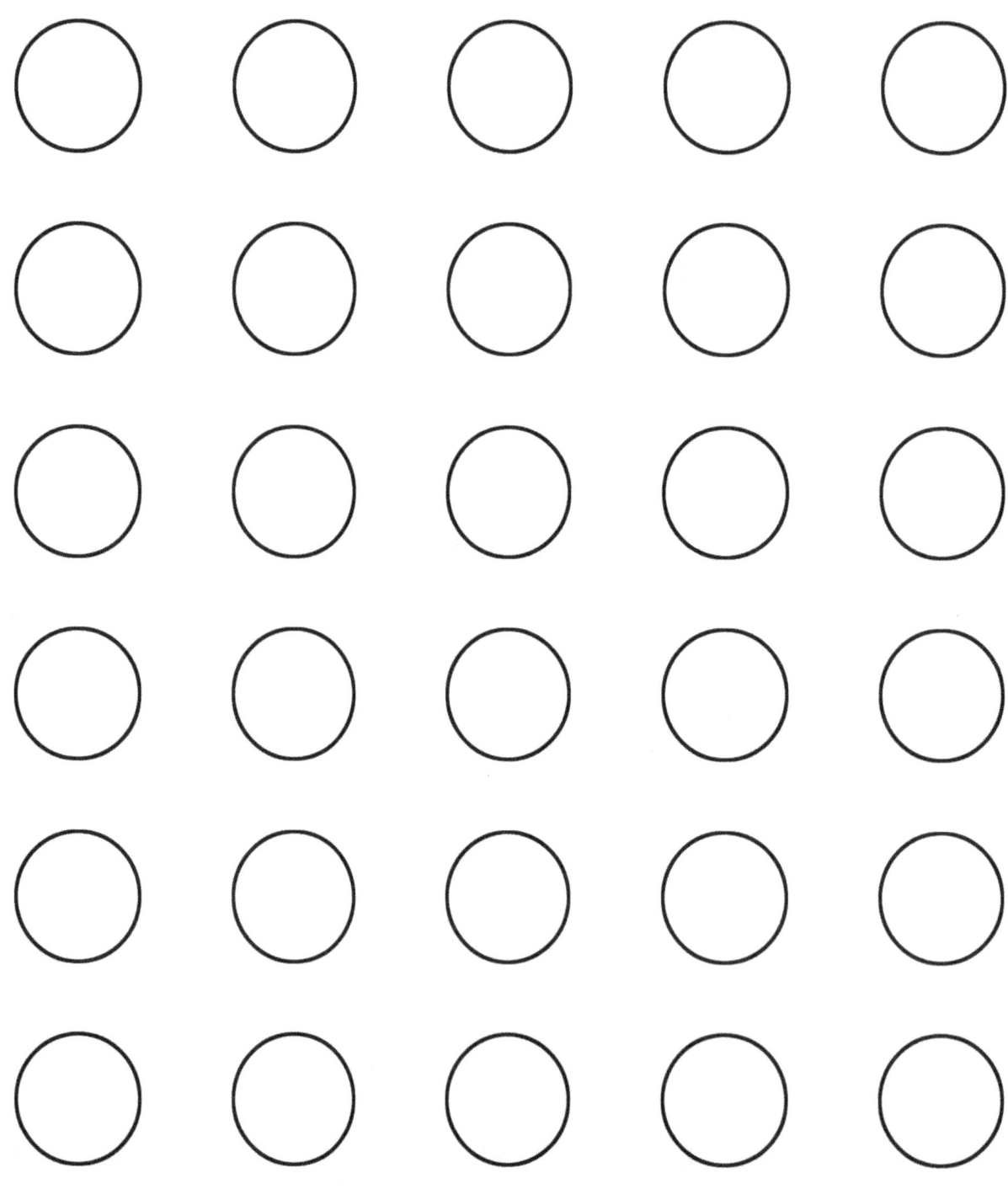

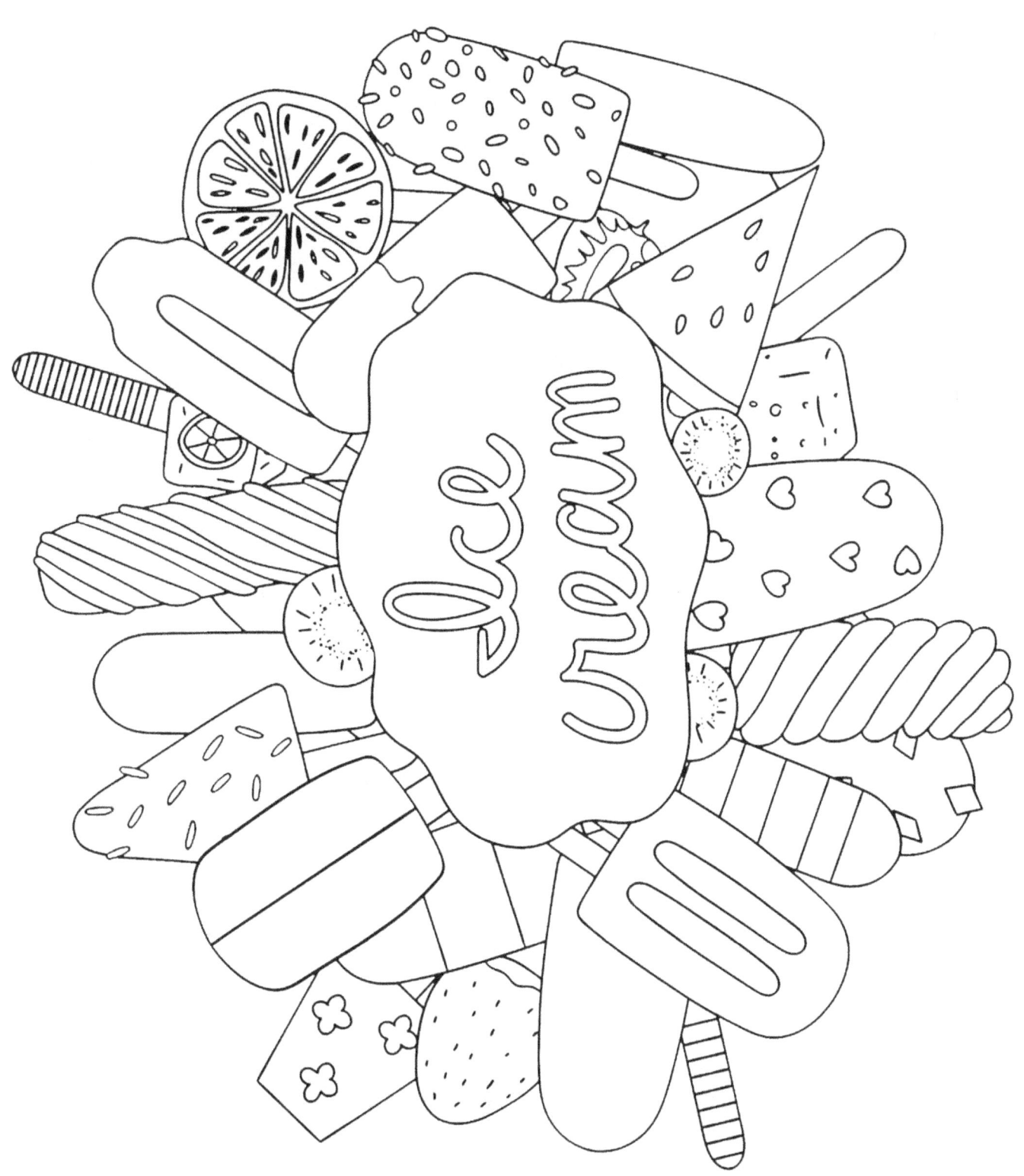

Test Your Color

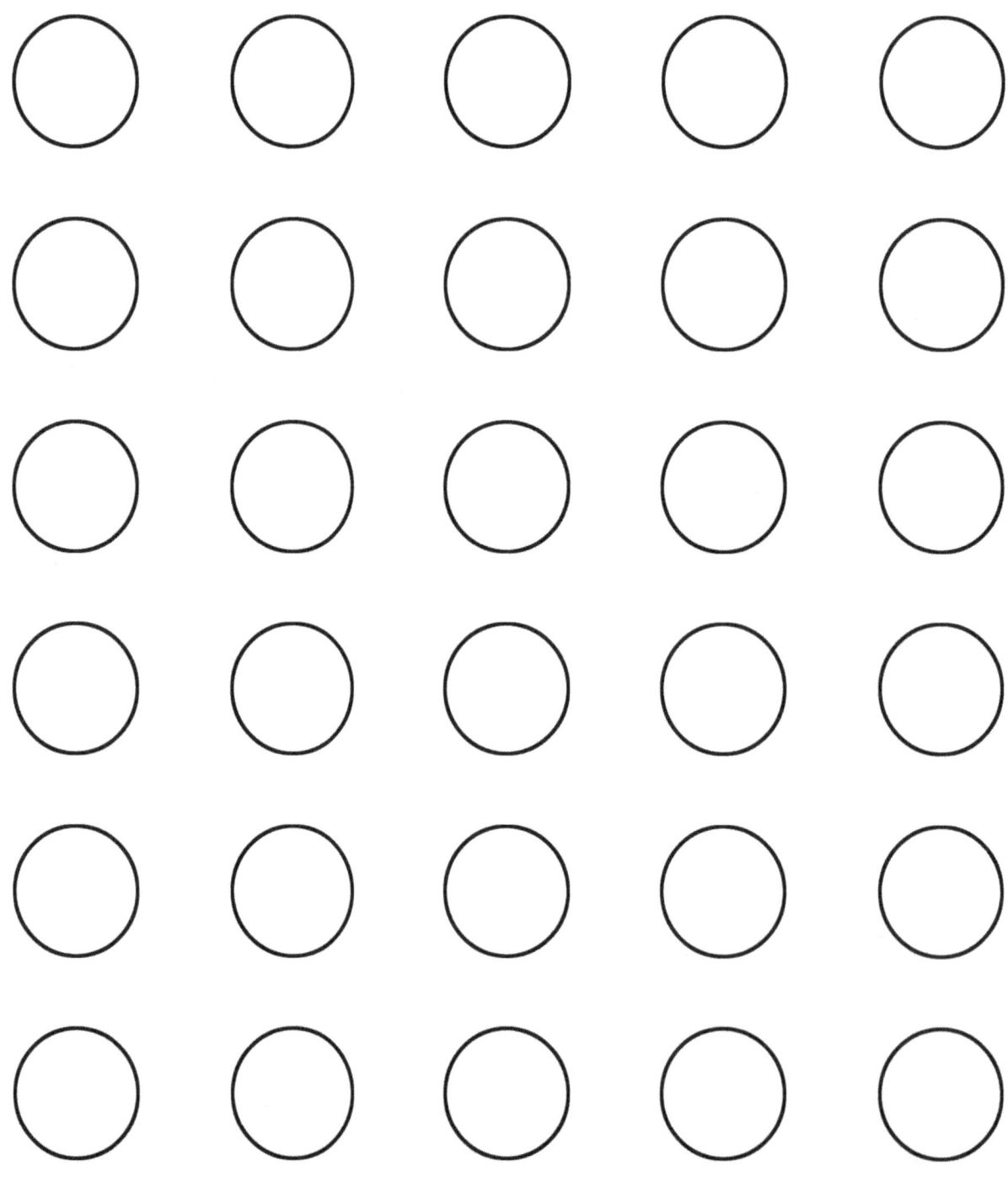

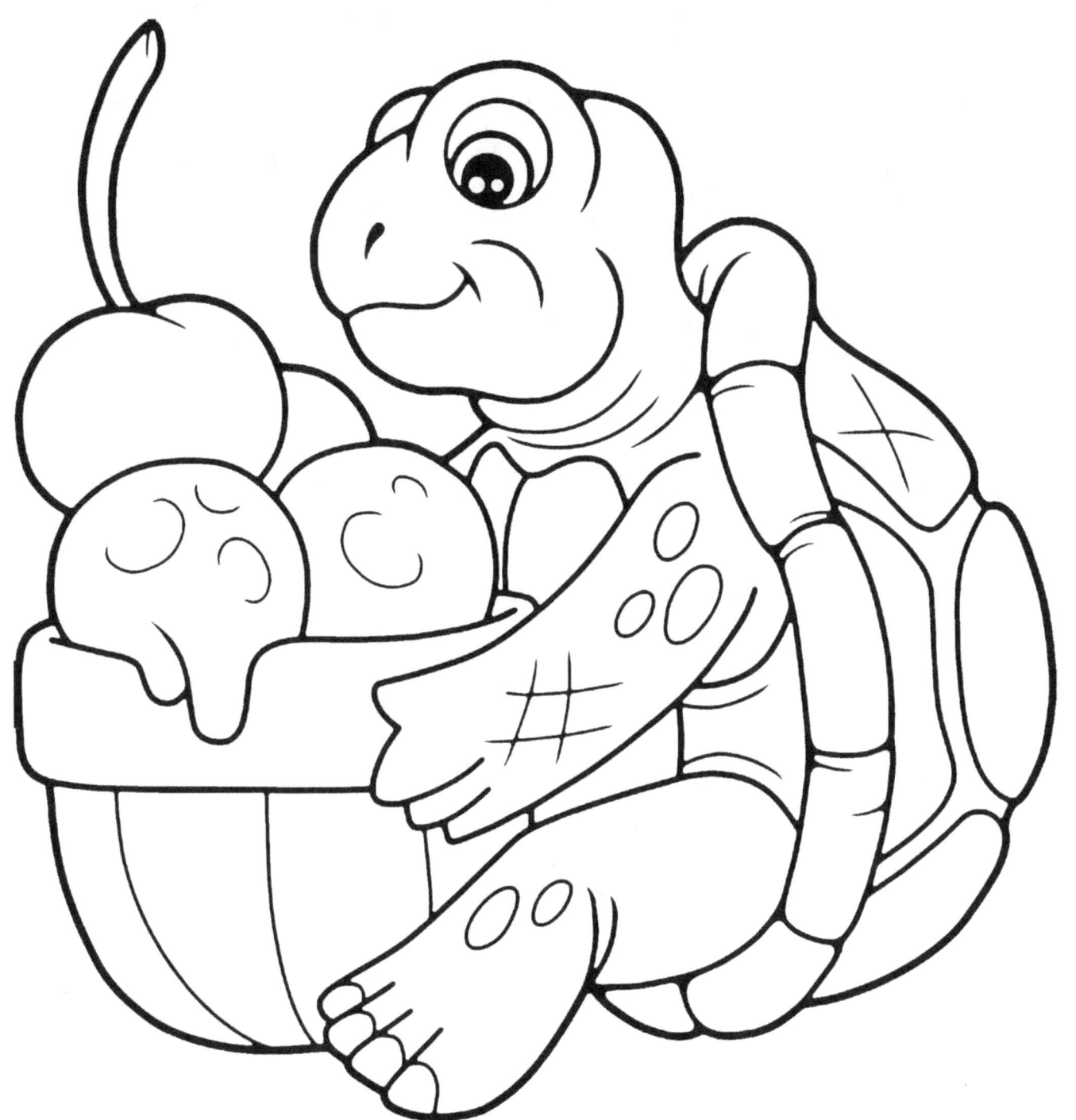

Test Your Color

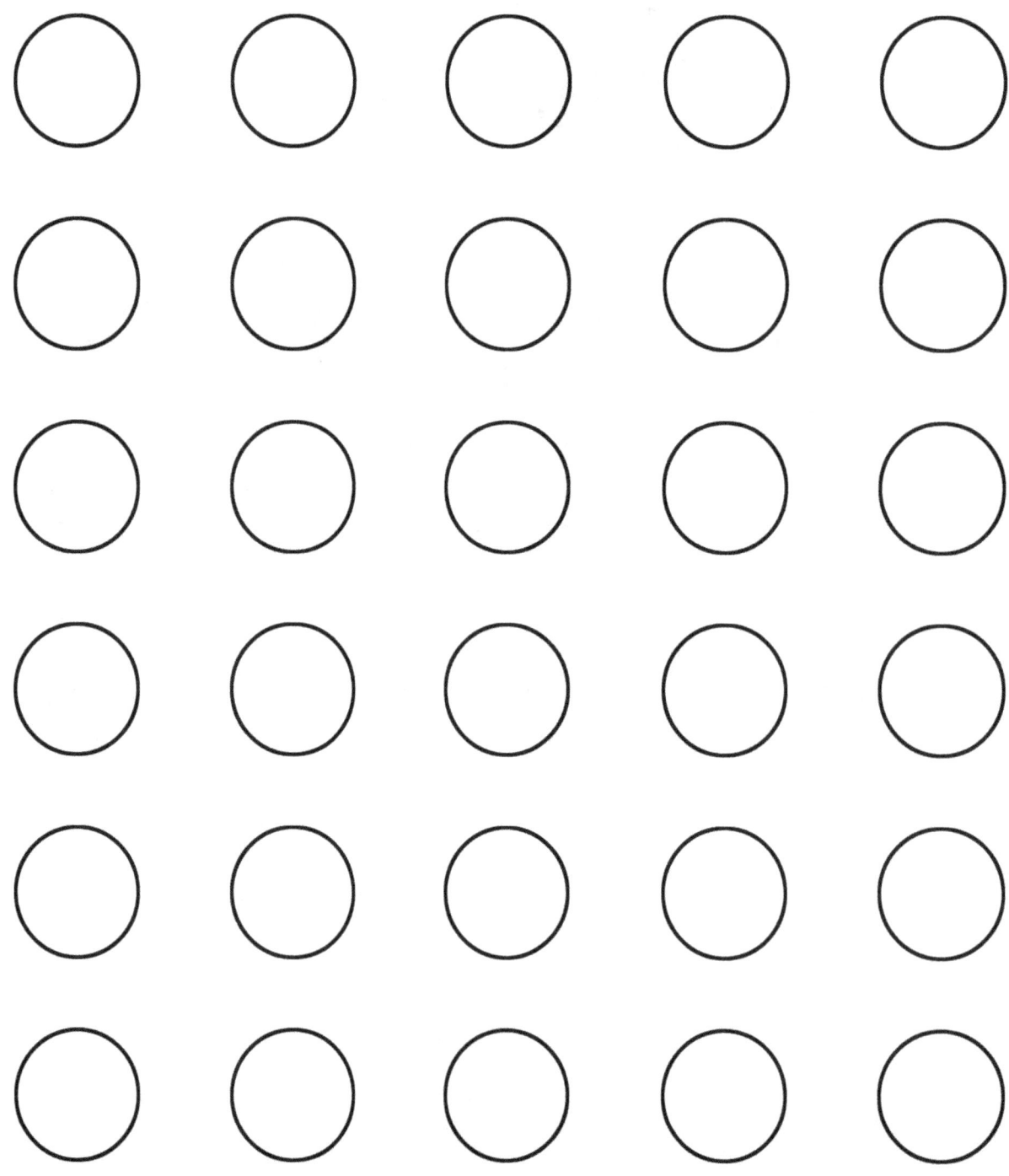

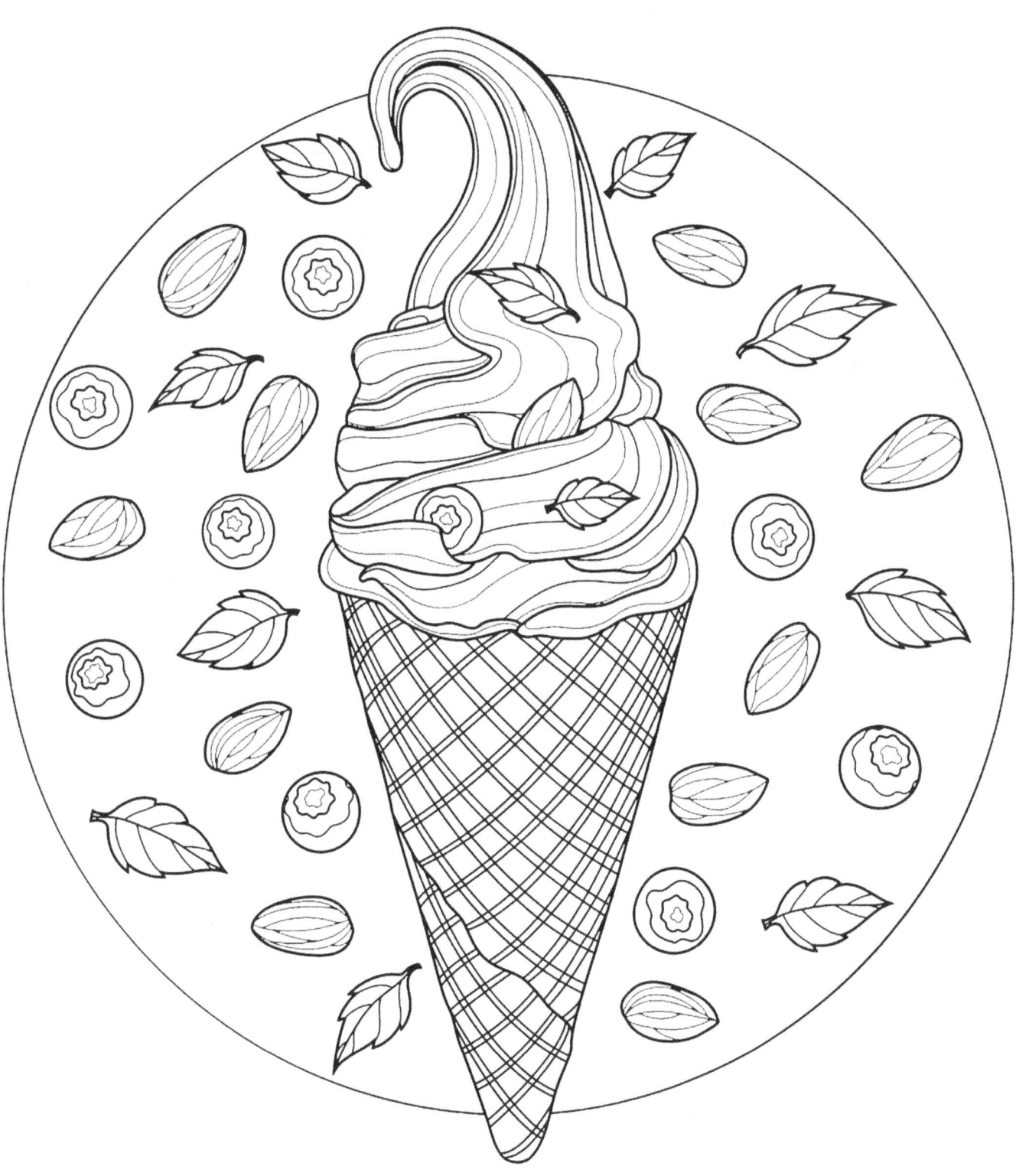

Test Your Color

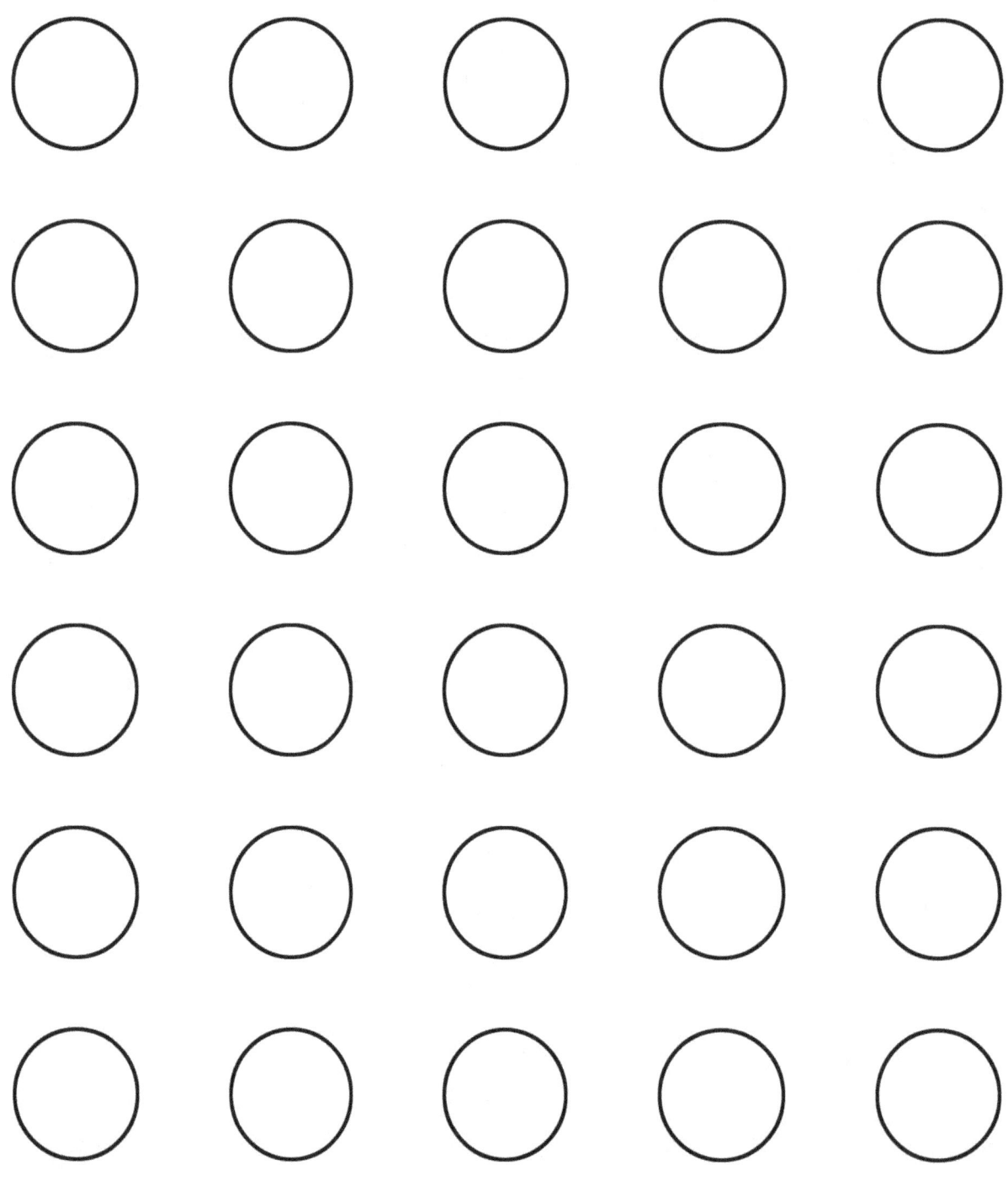

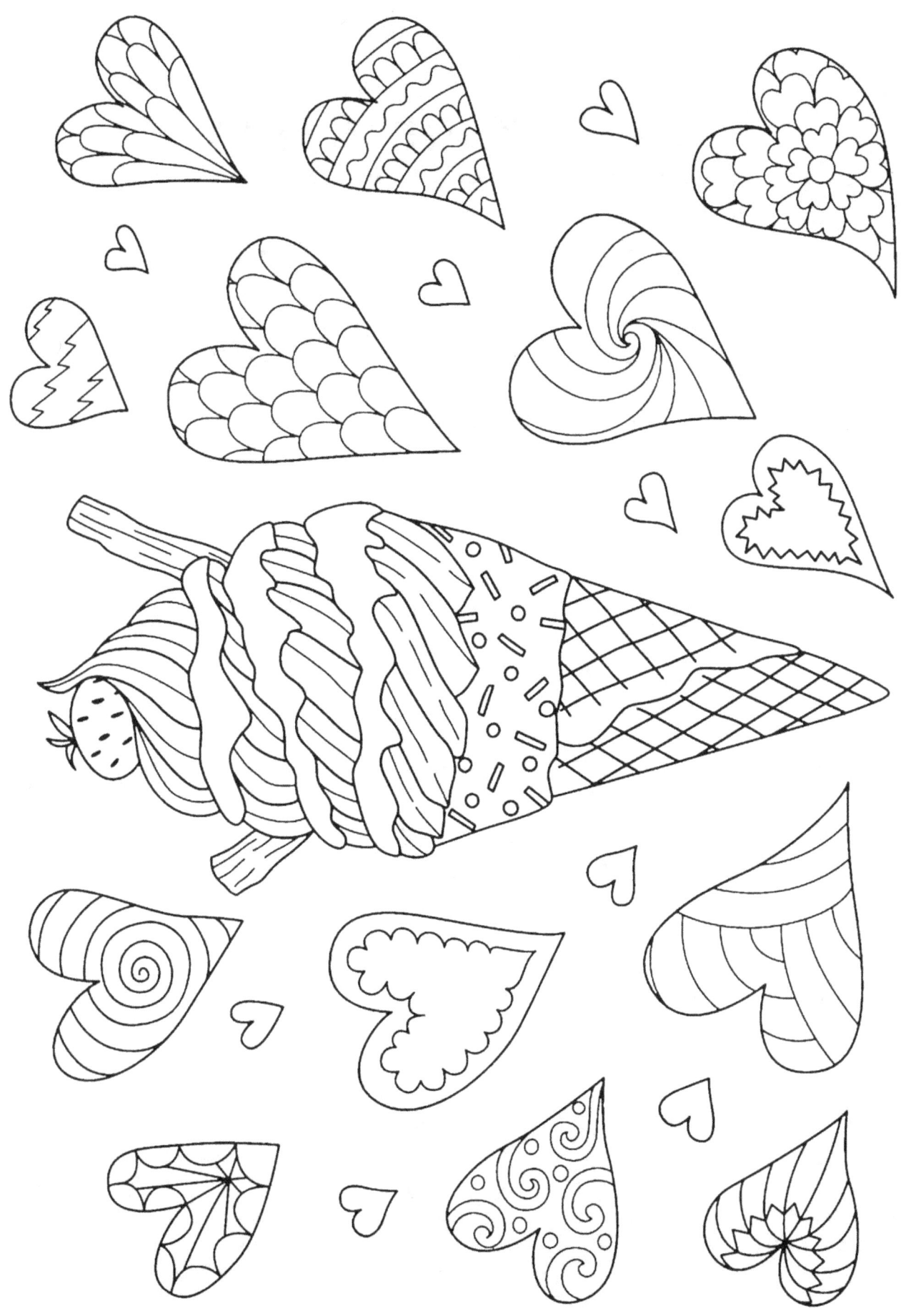

Test Your Color

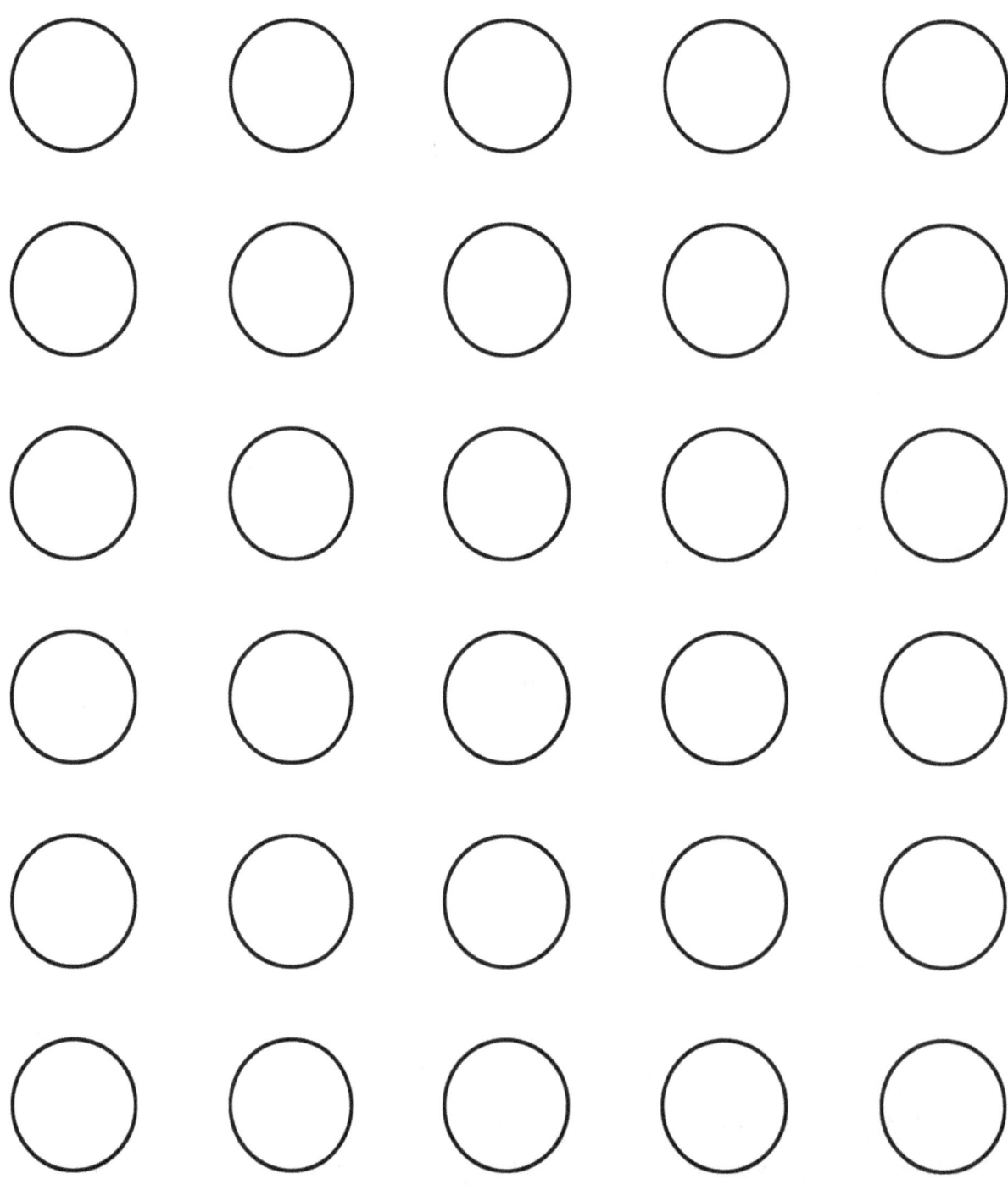

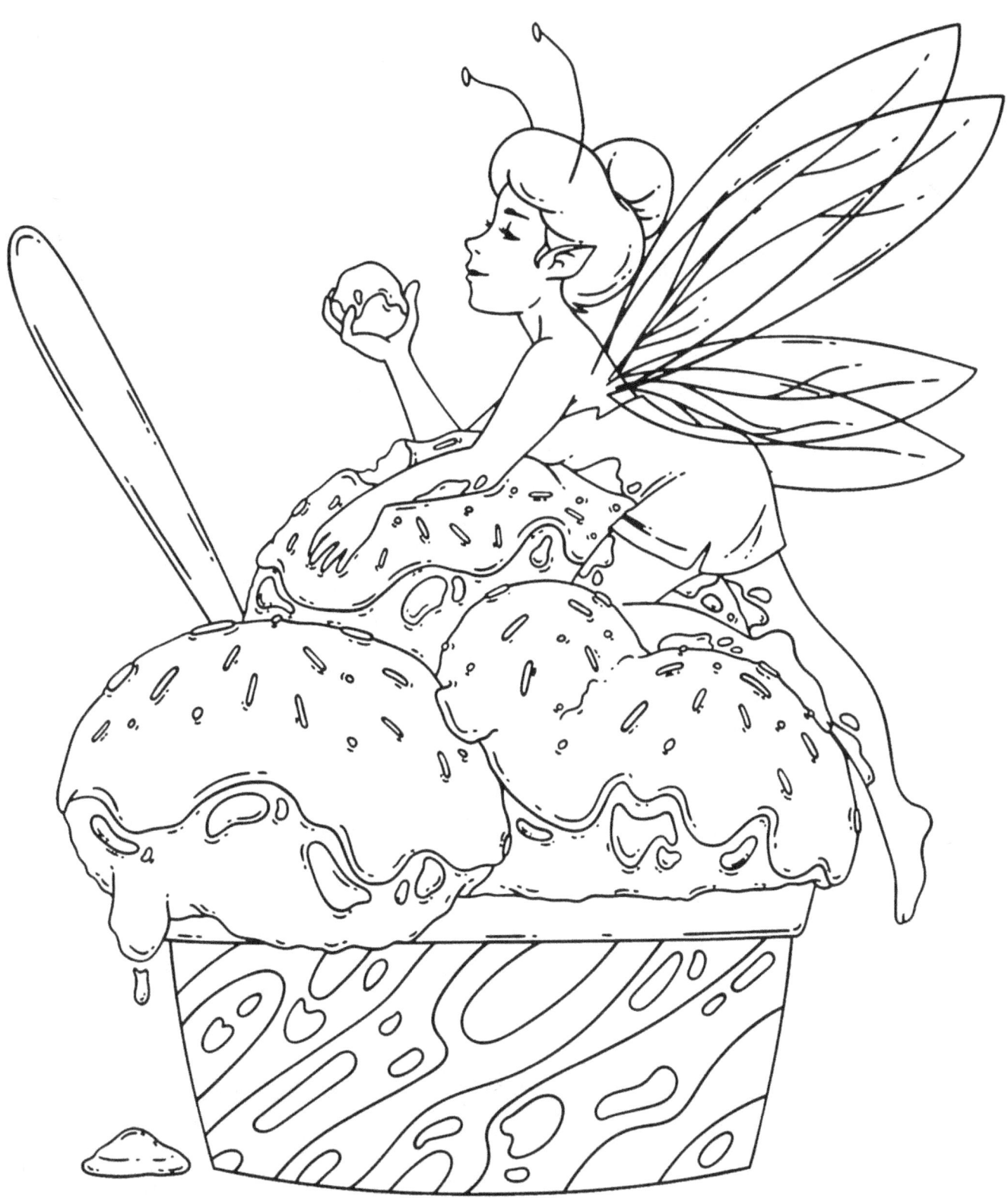

Test Your Color

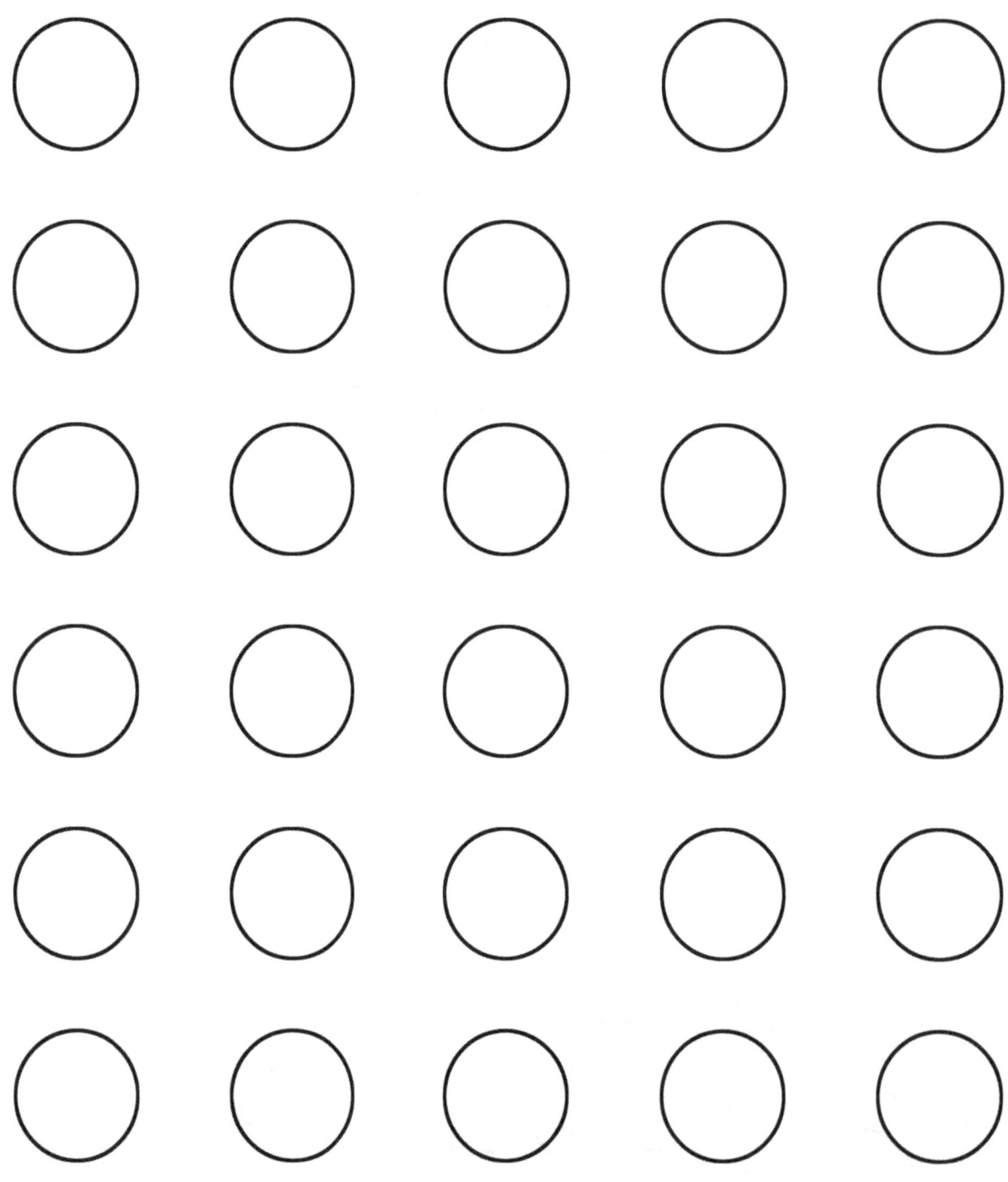

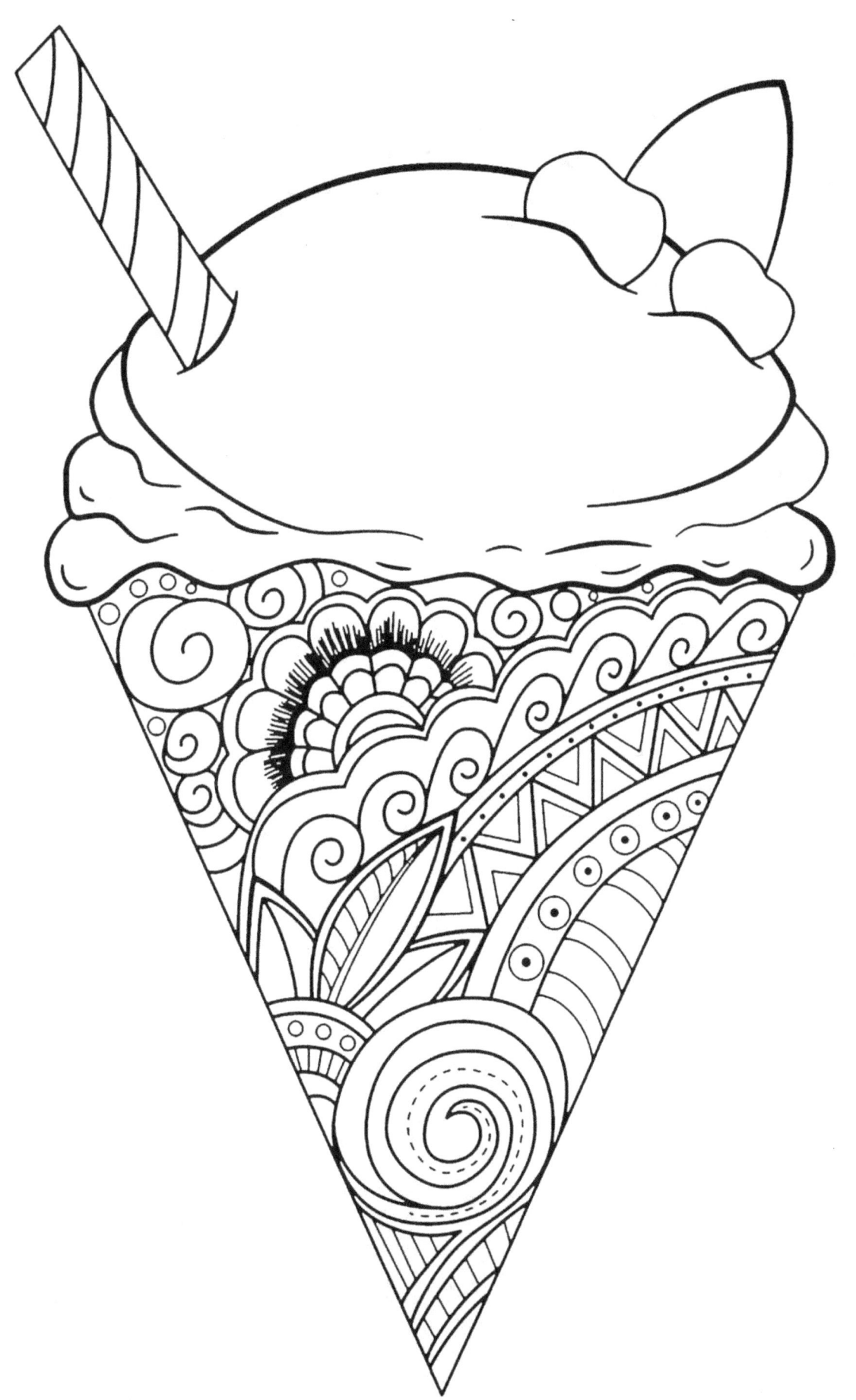

Test Your Color

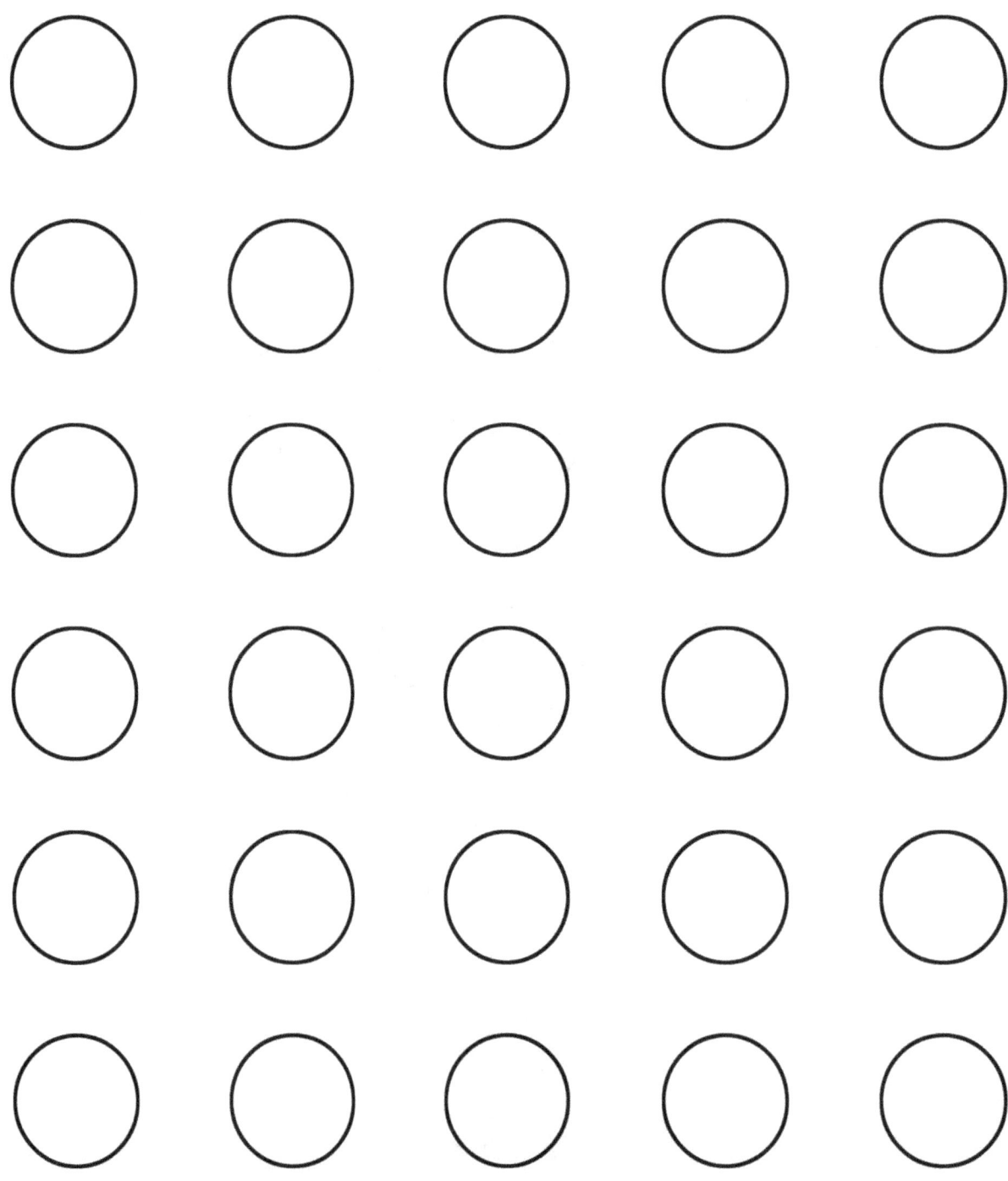

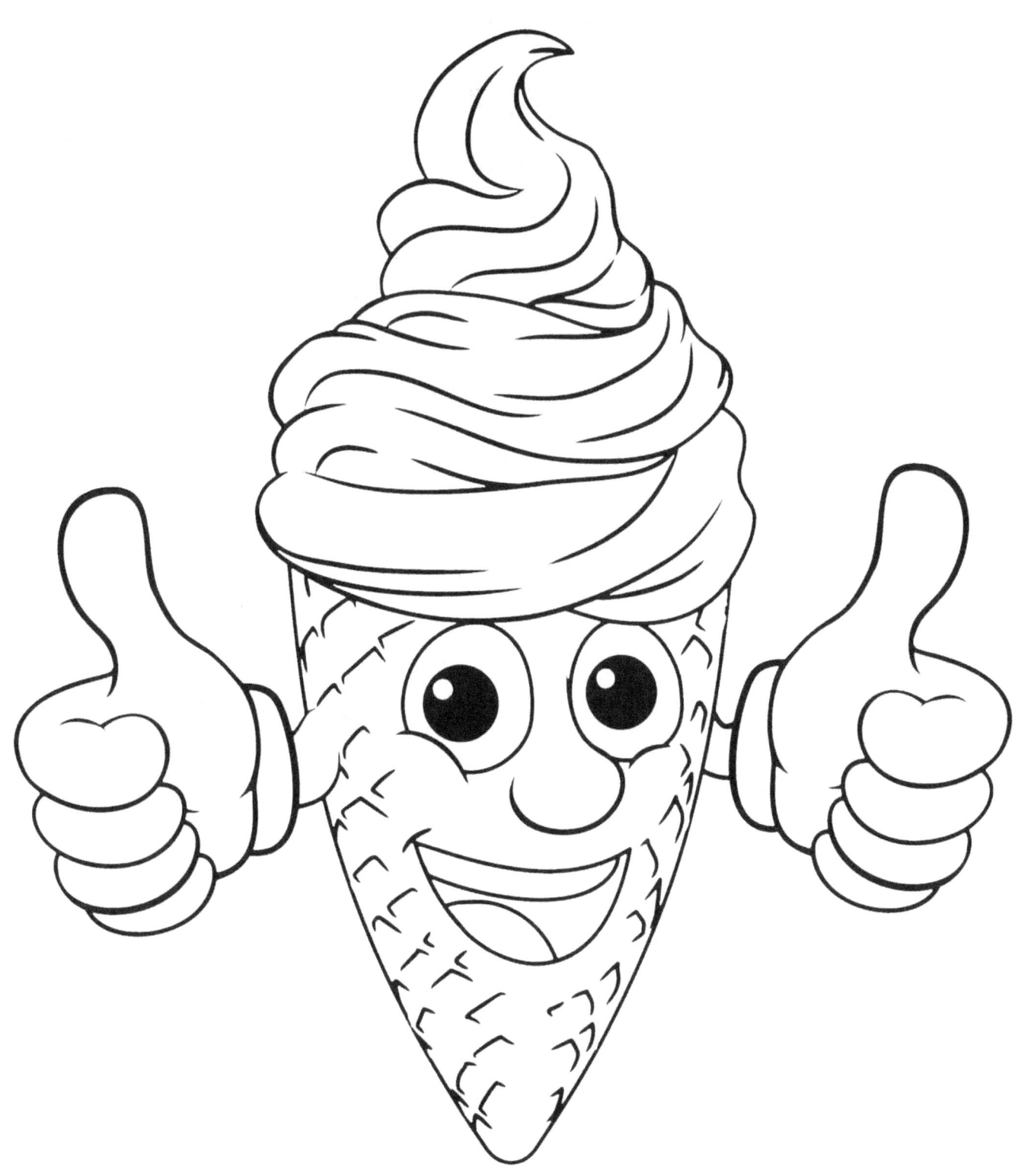

Test Your Color

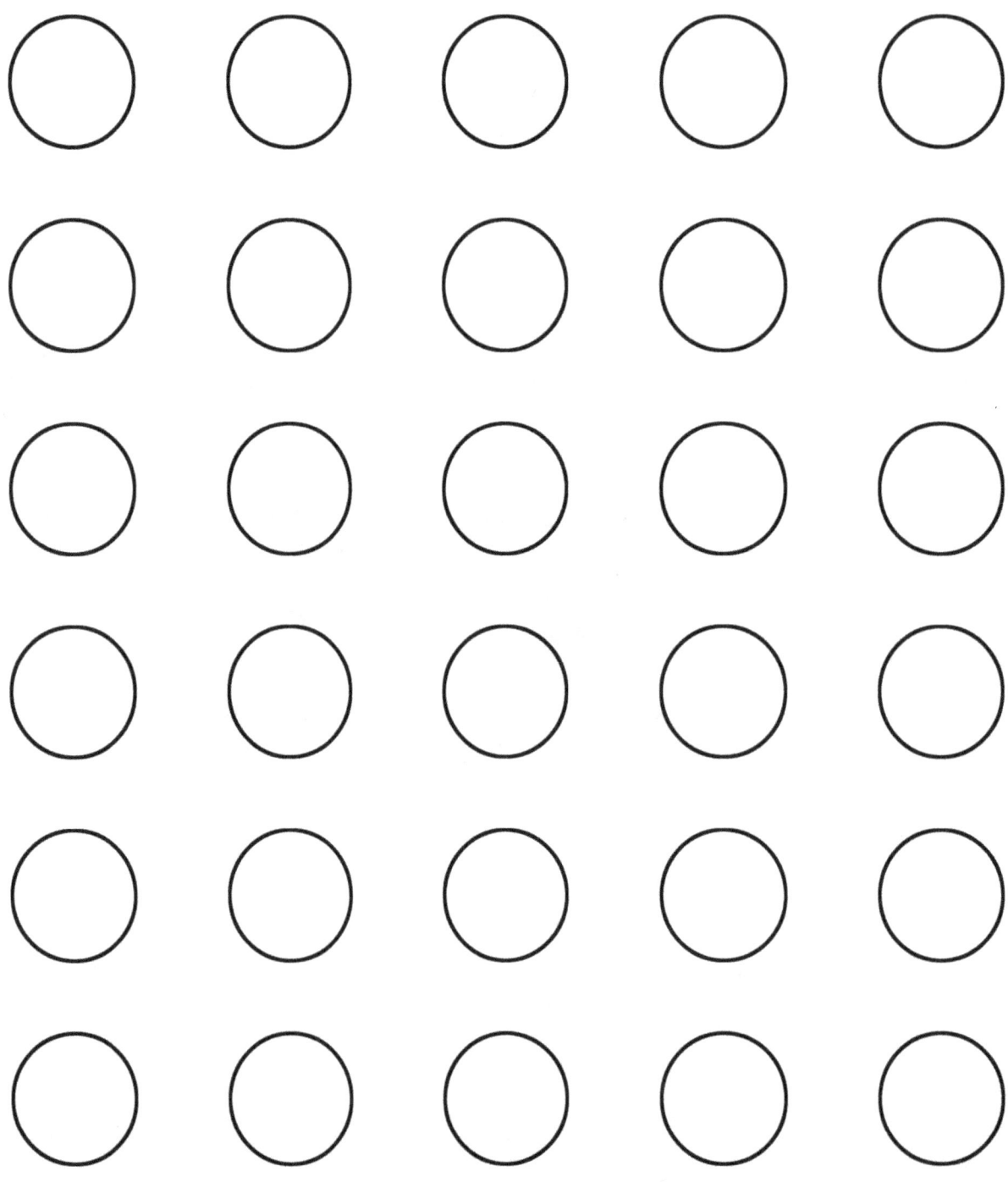

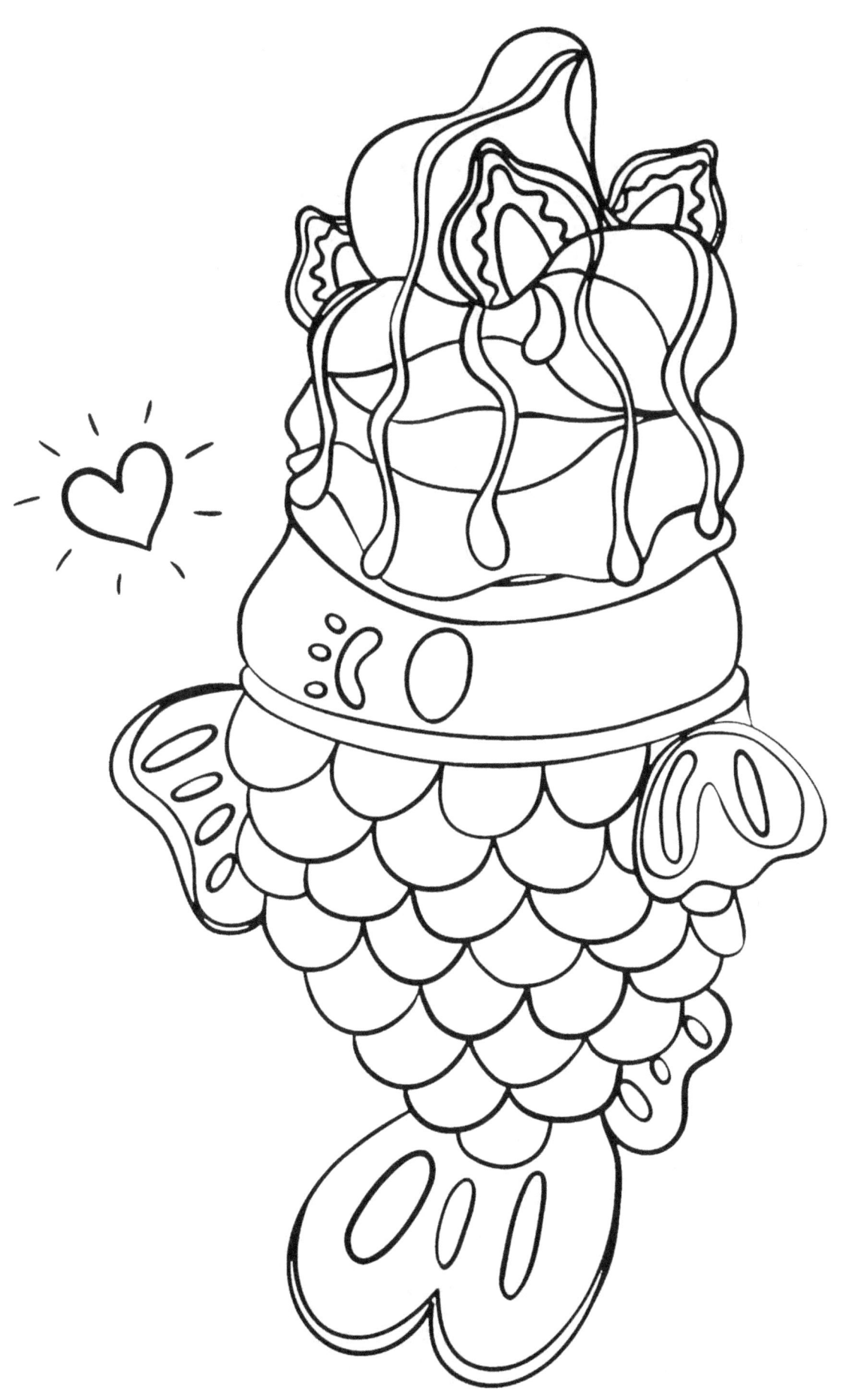

Test Your Color

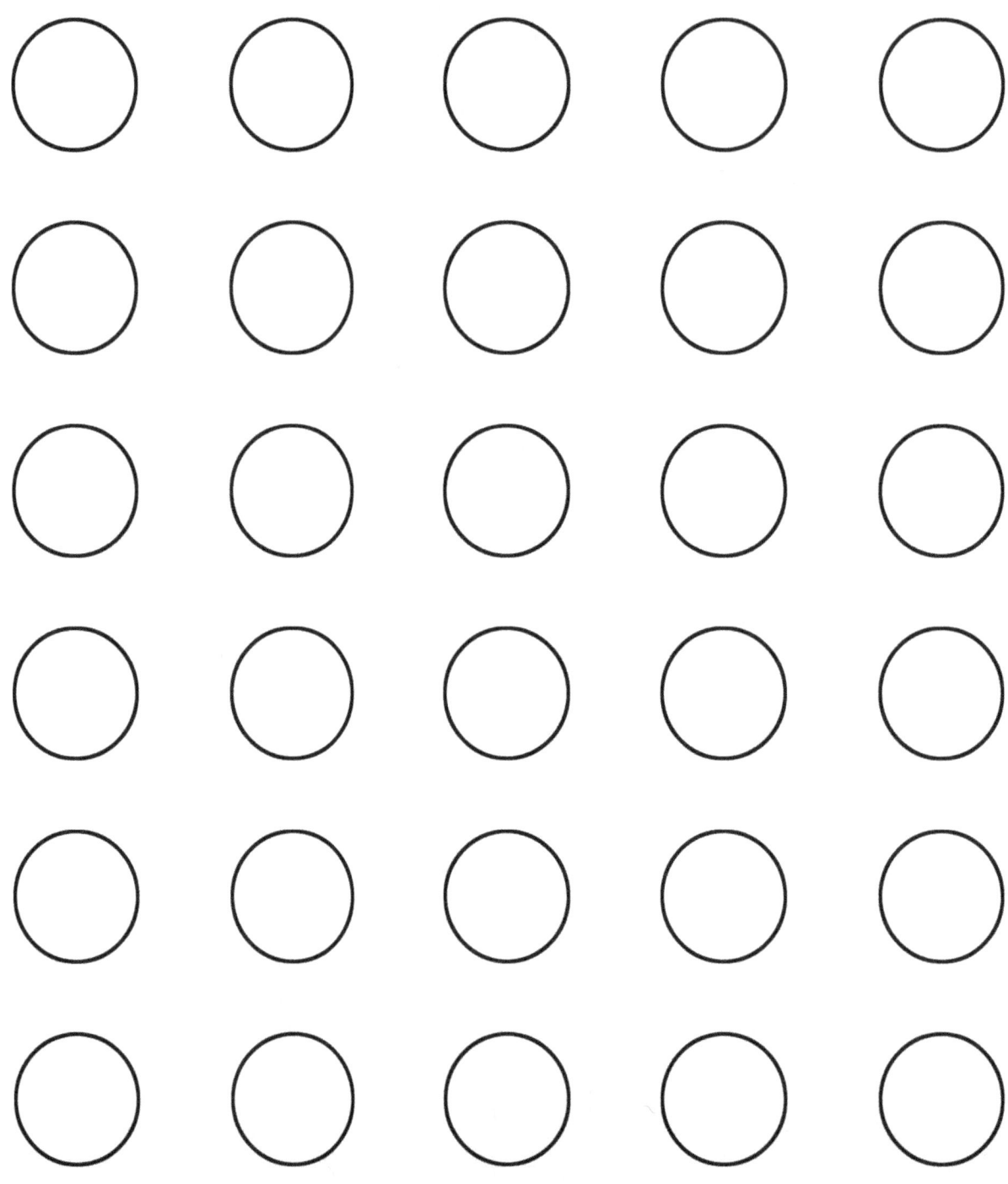

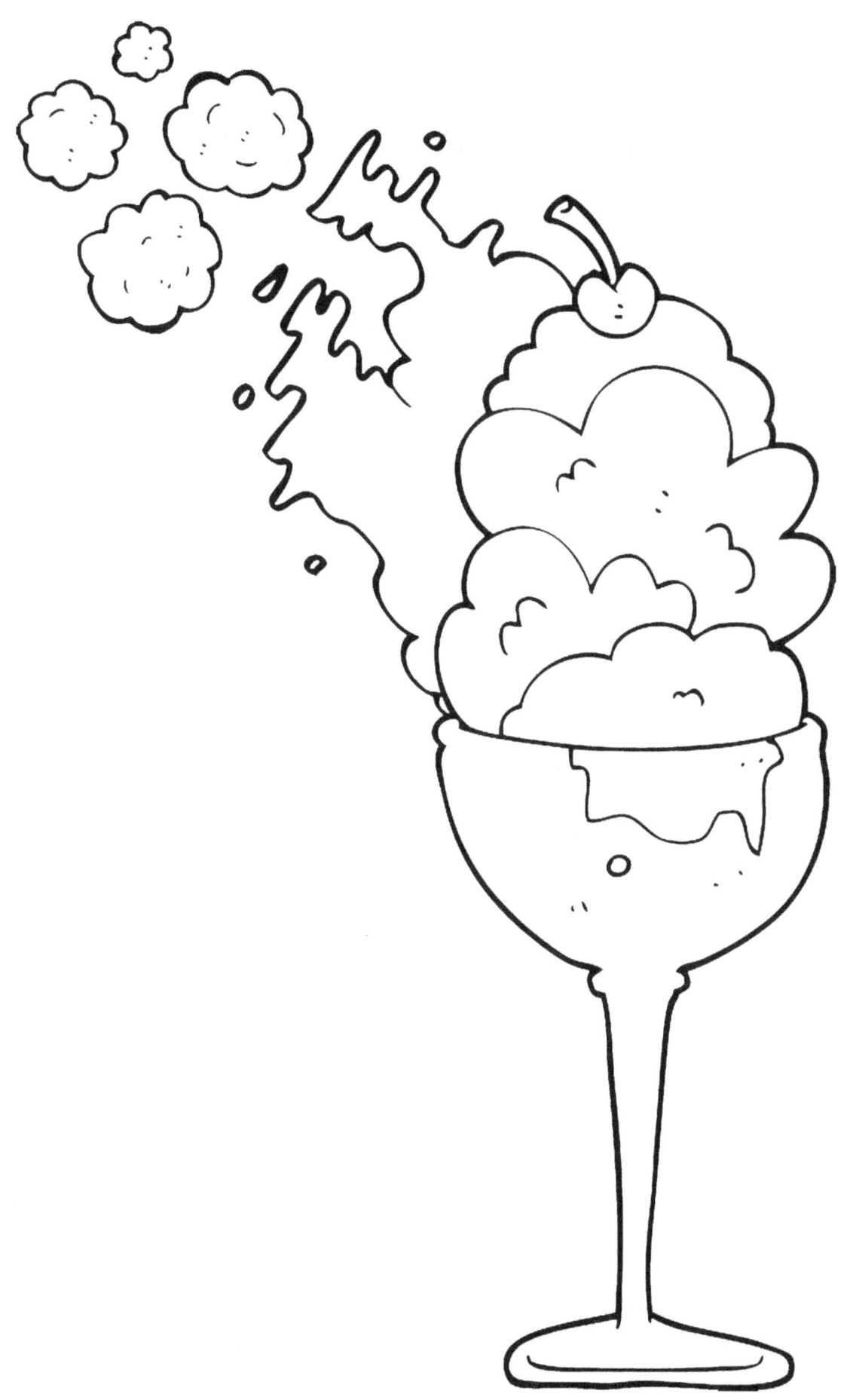

Test Your Color

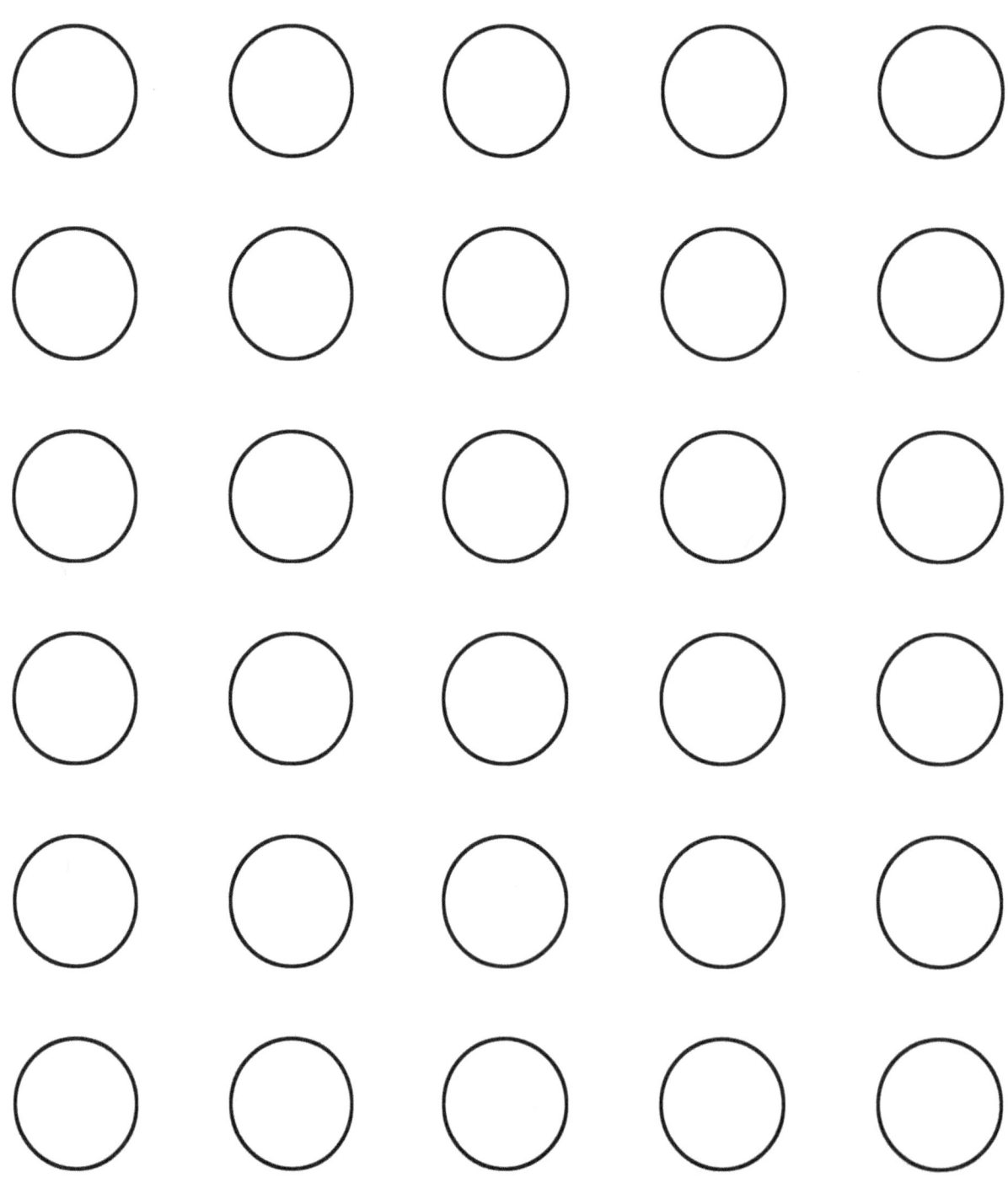

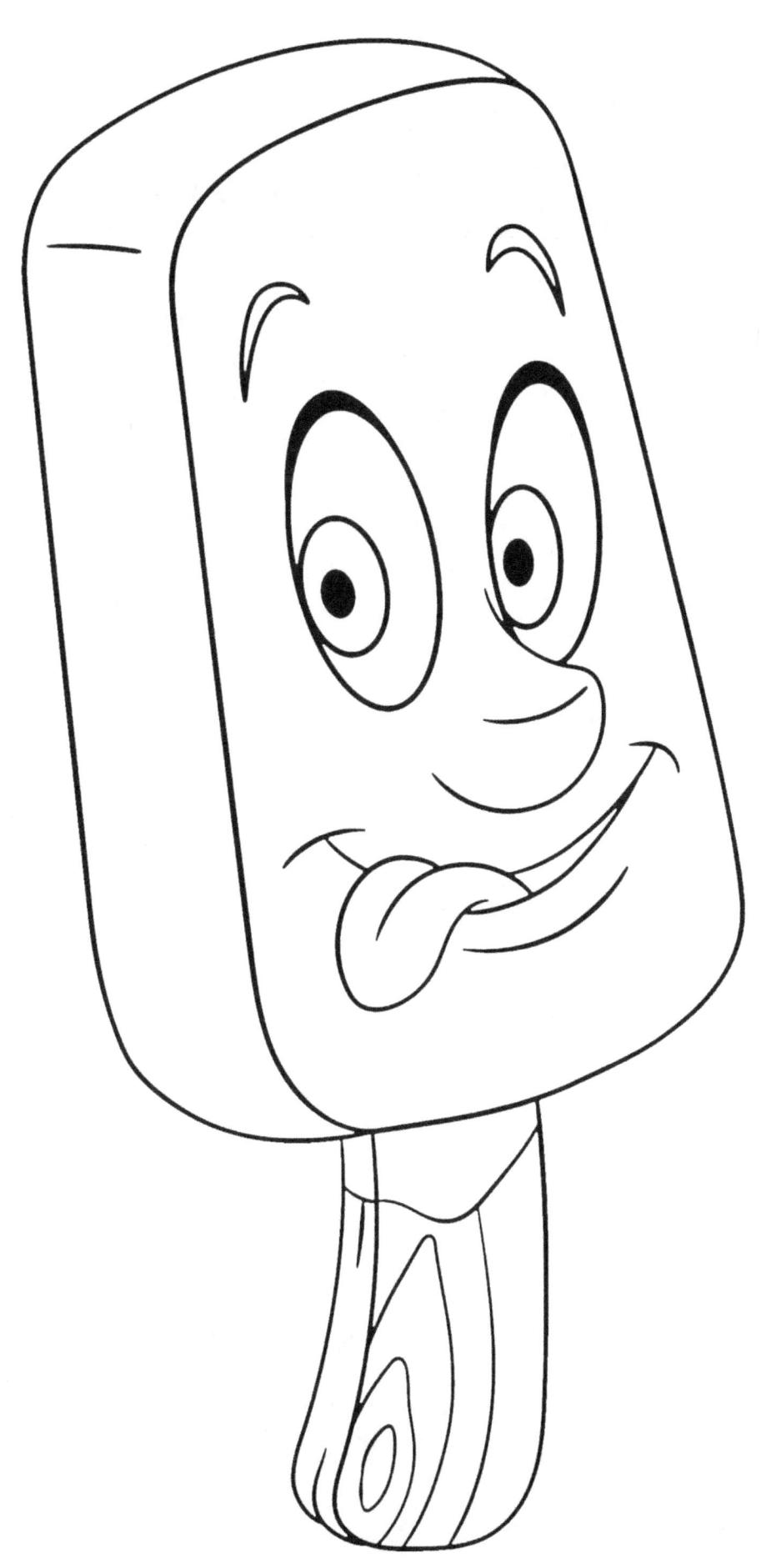

Test Your Color

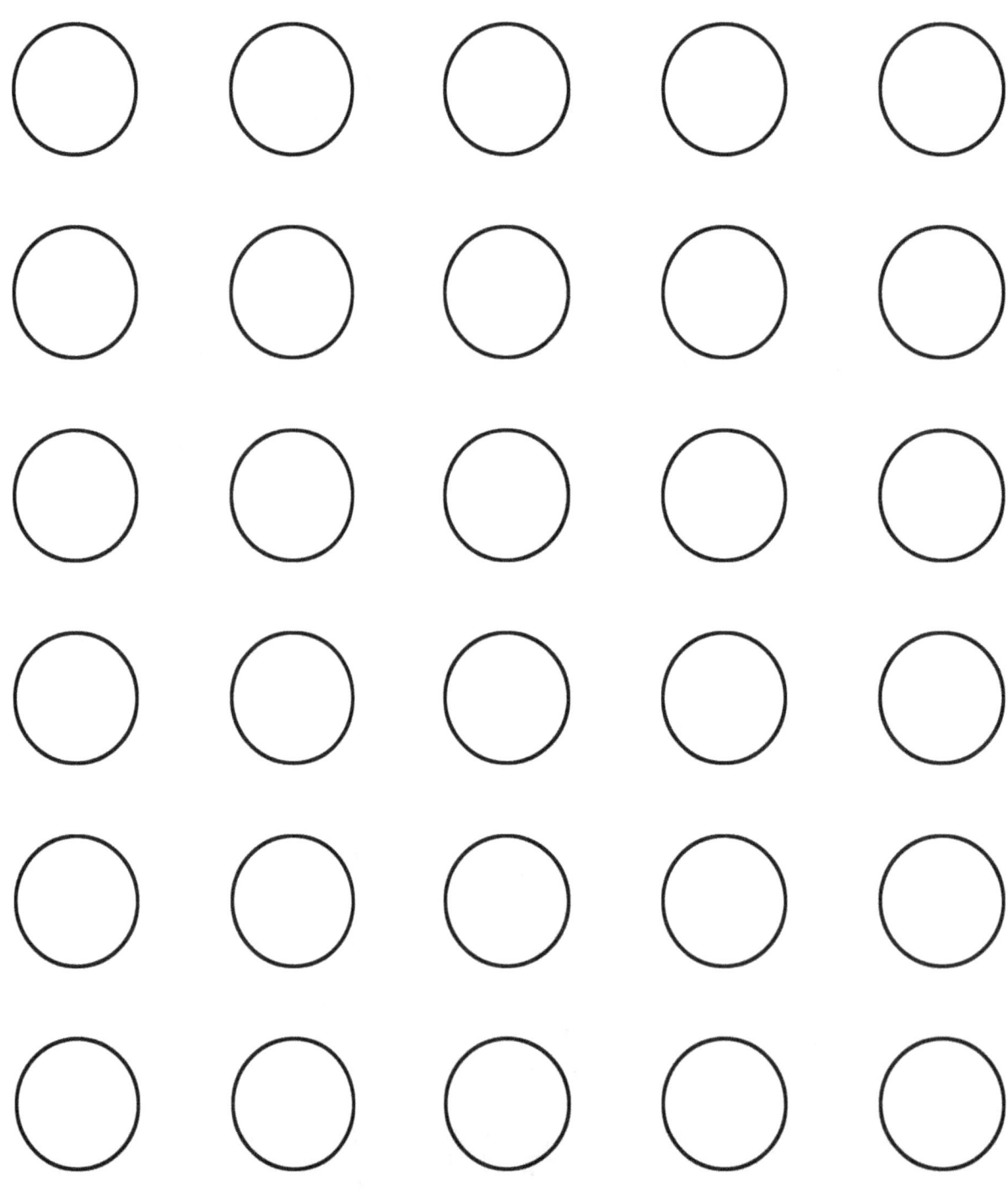

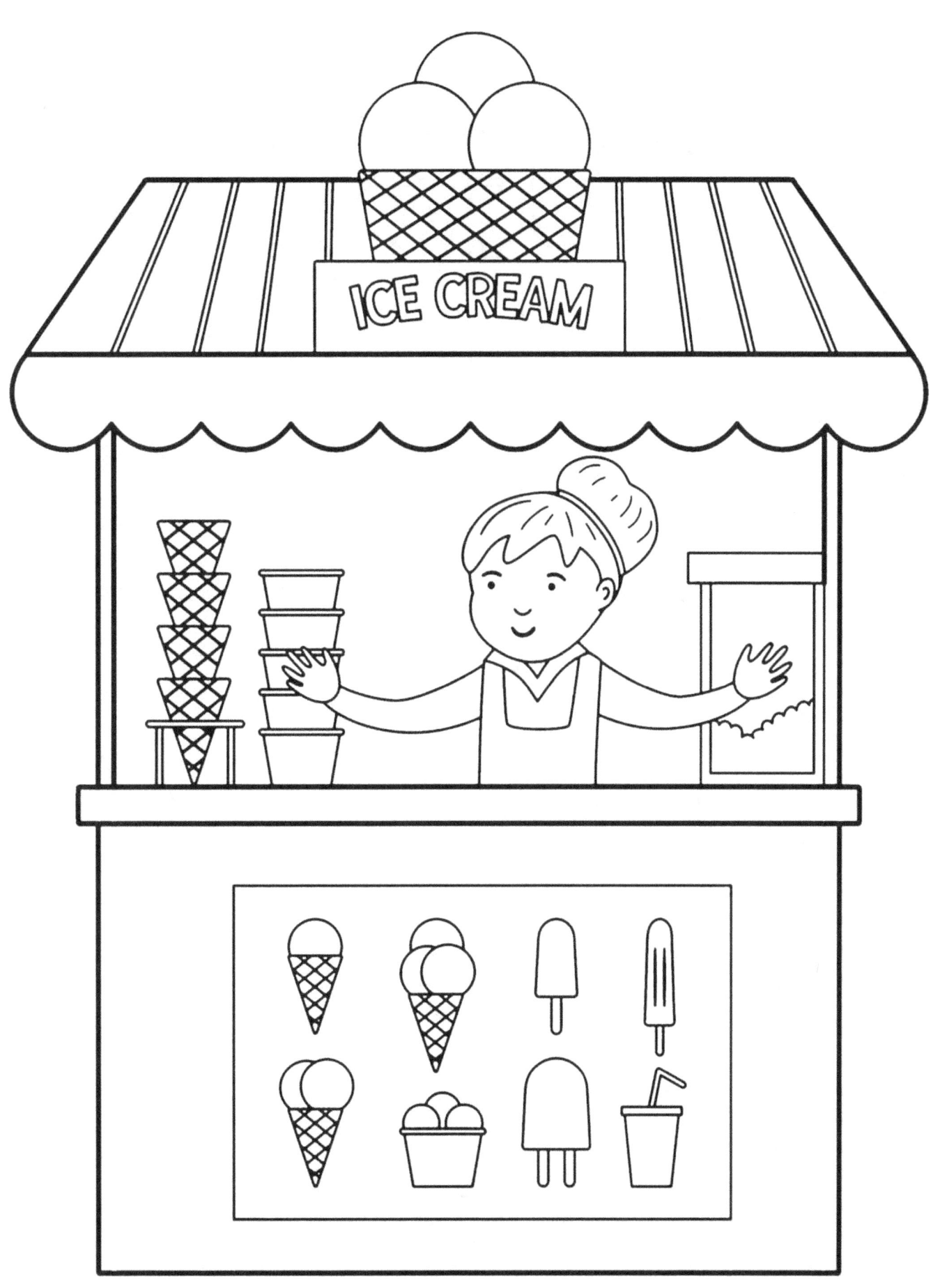

Test Your Color

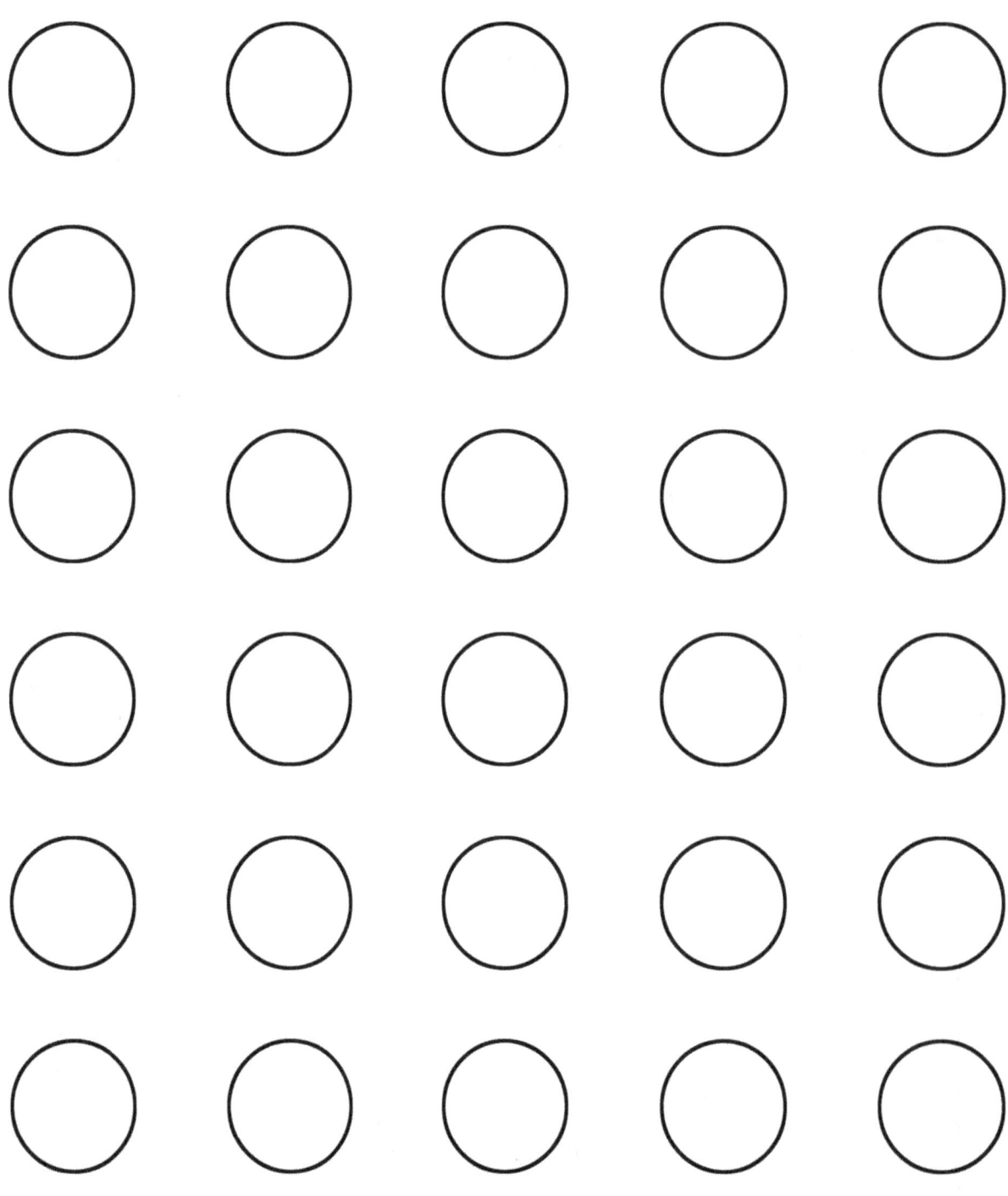

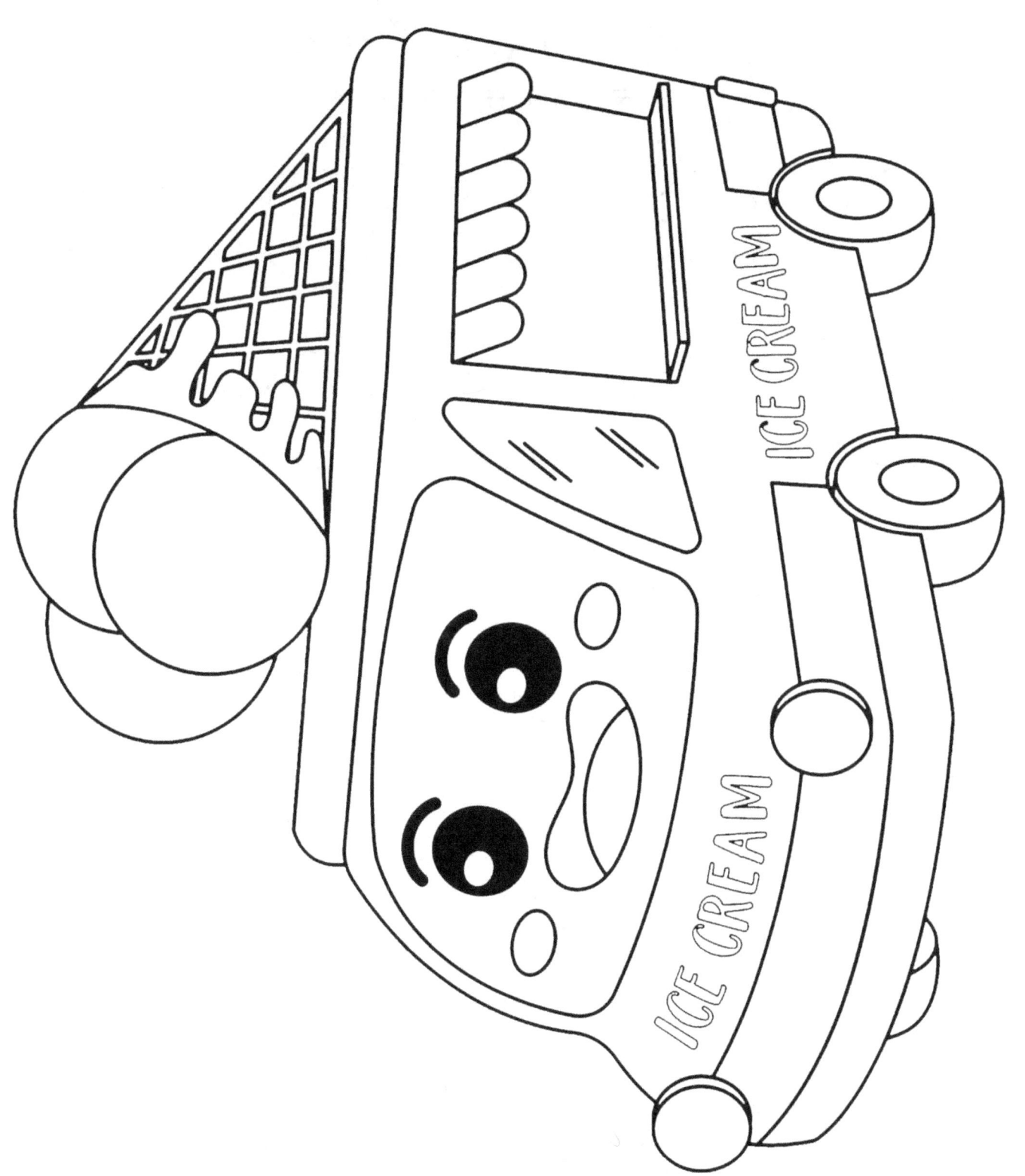

Test Your Color

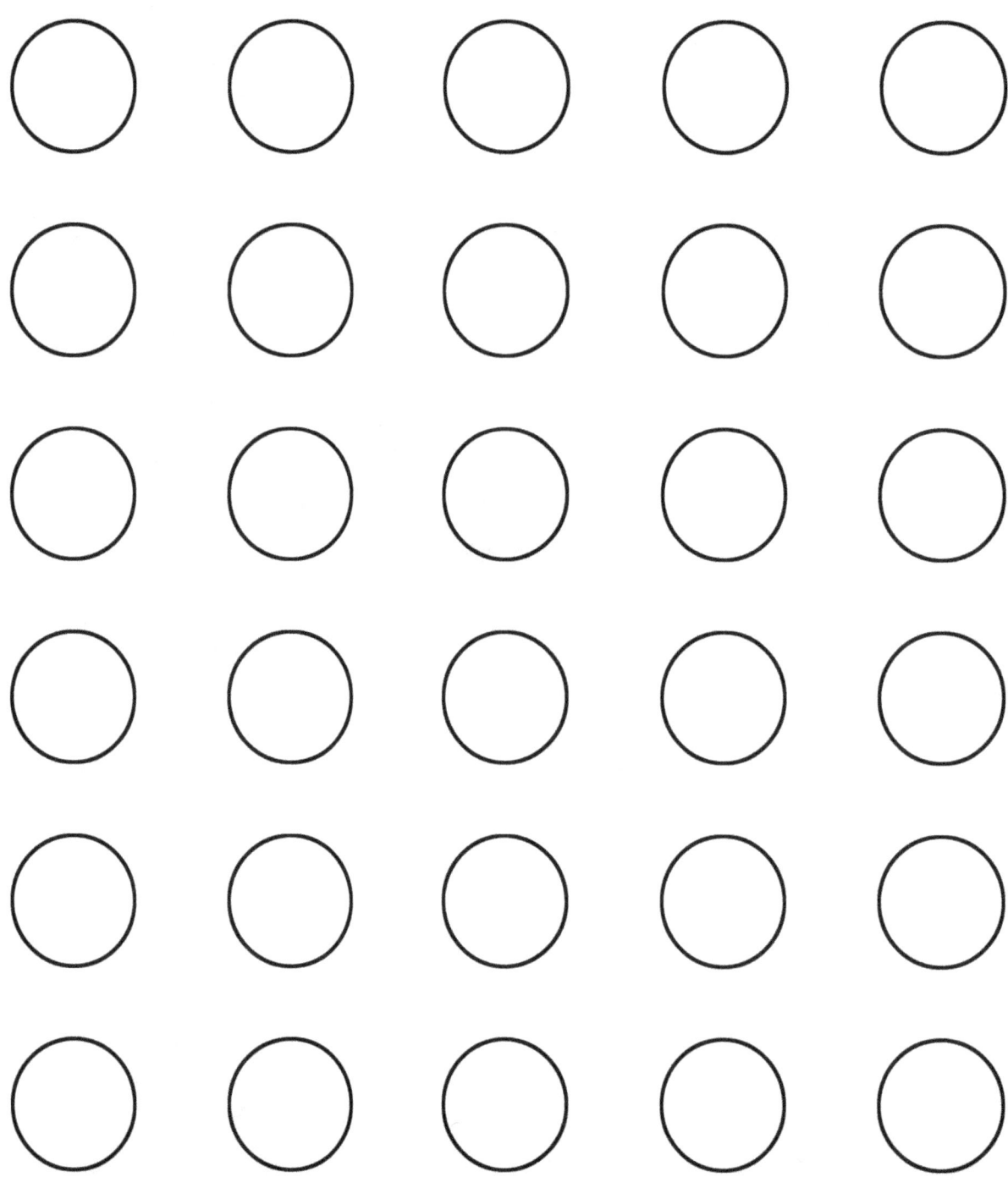

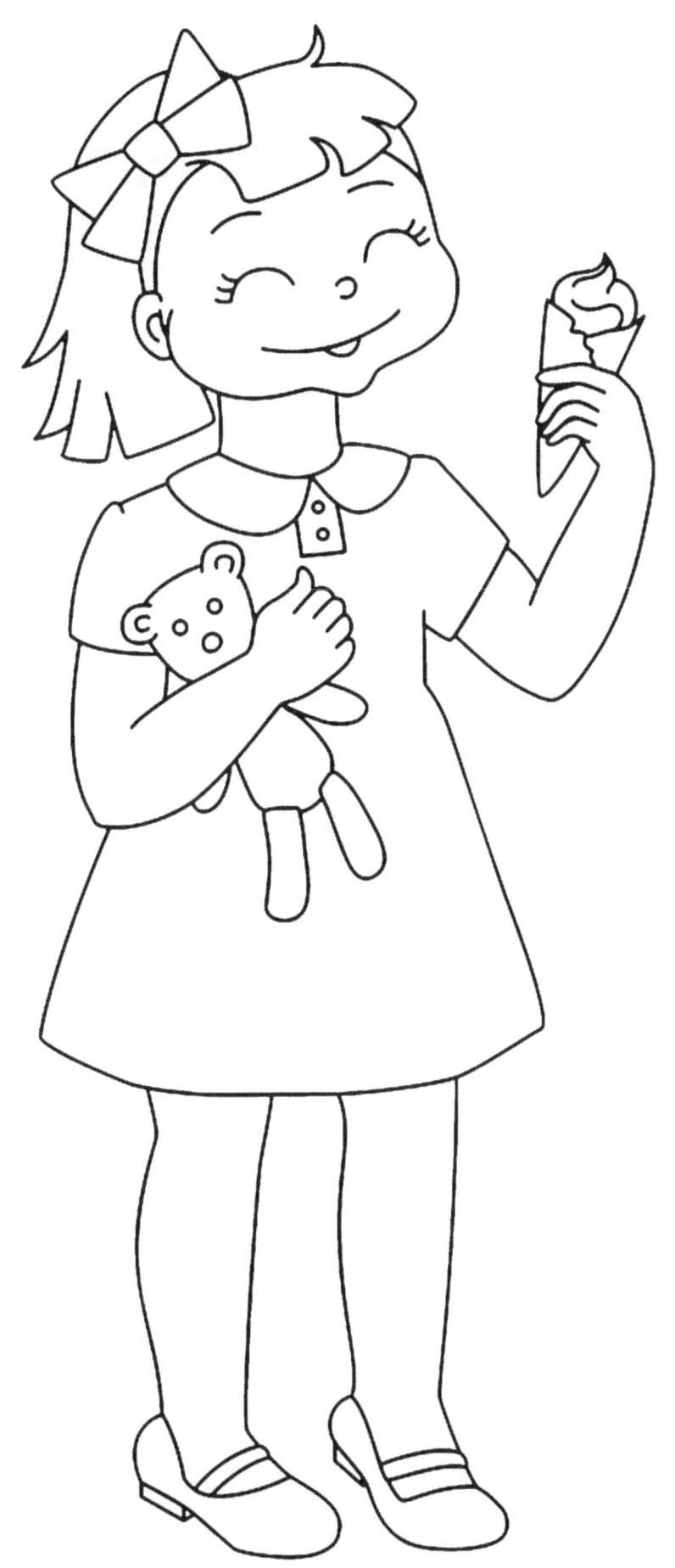

Test Your Color

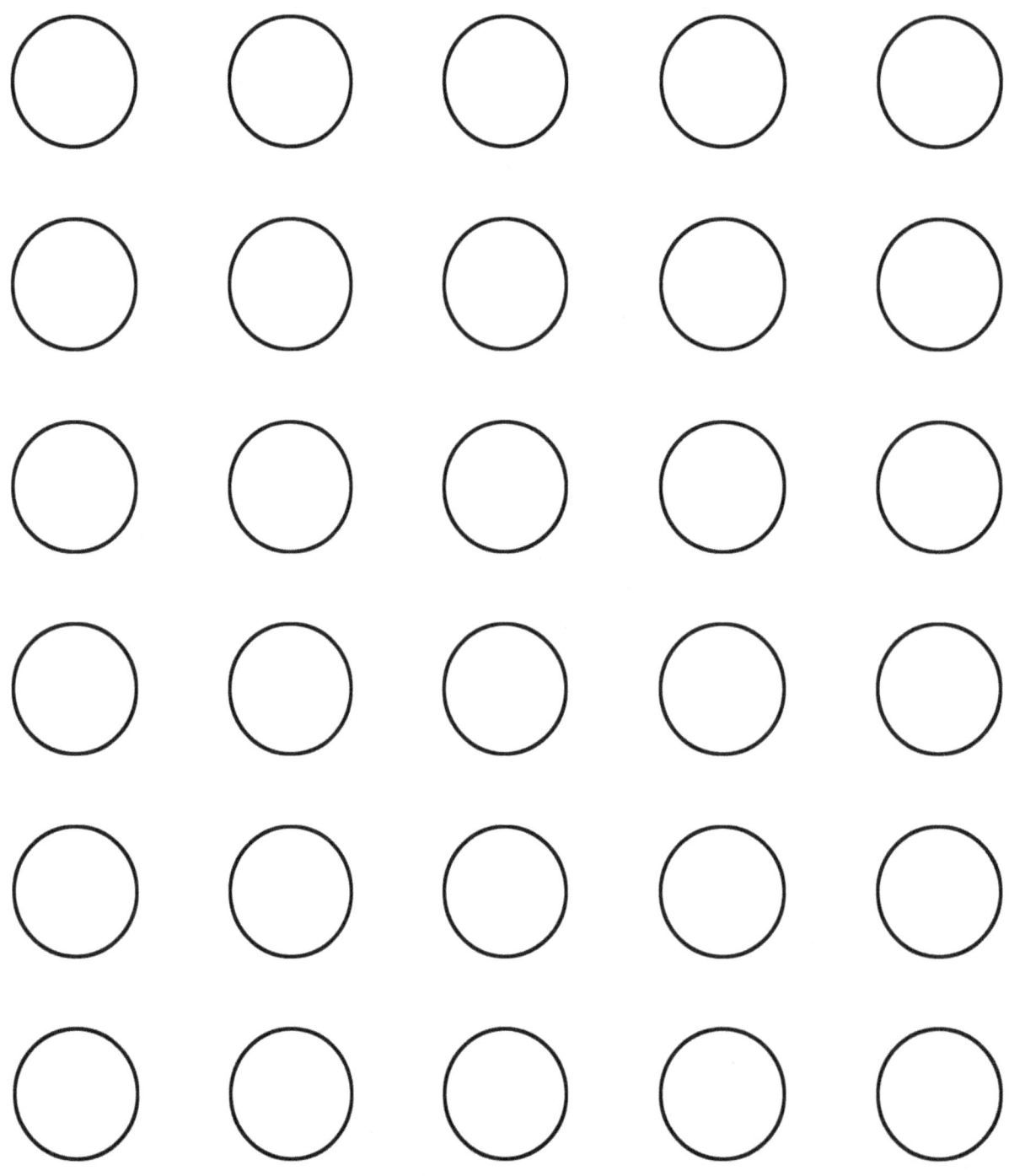

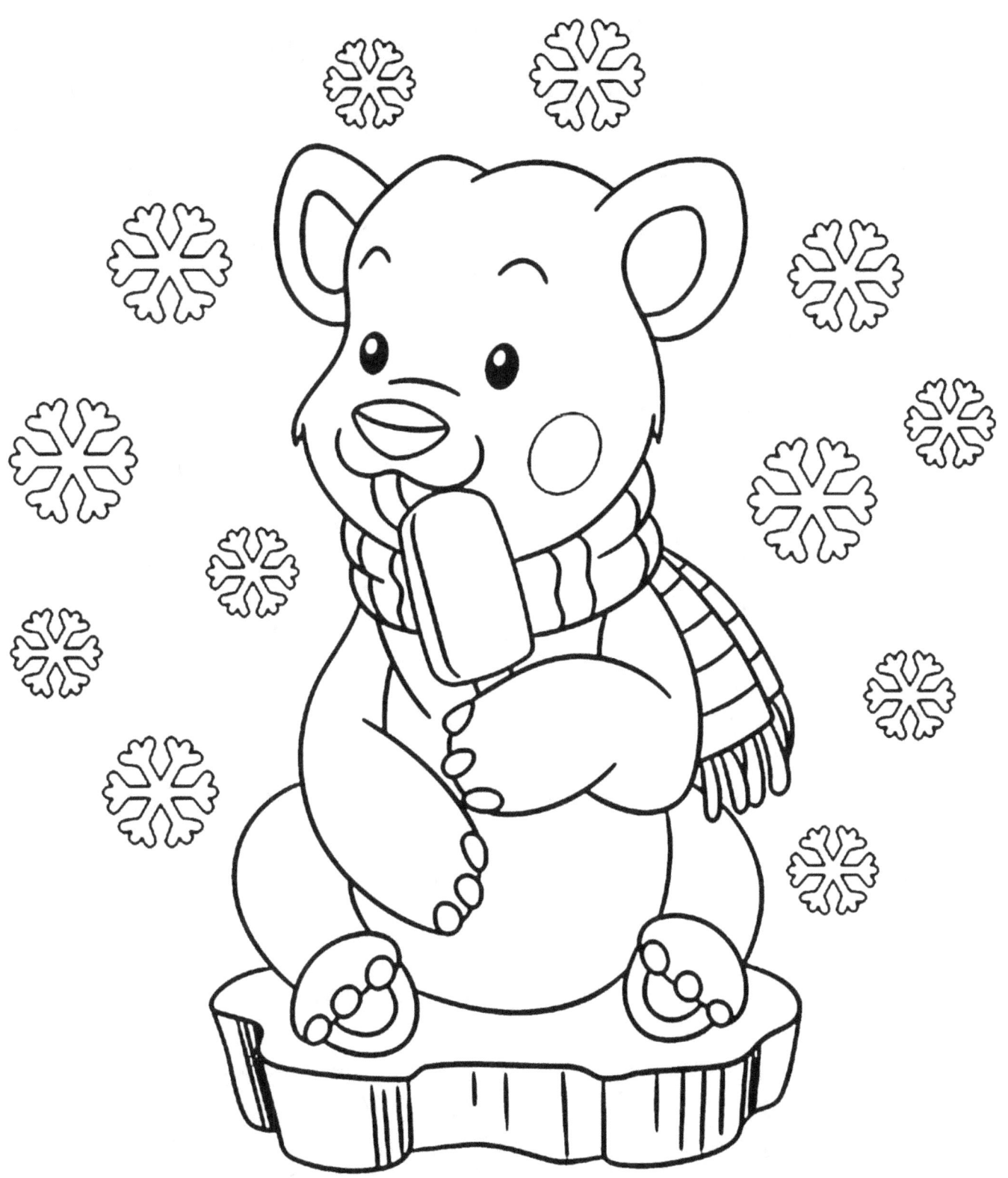

Test Your Color

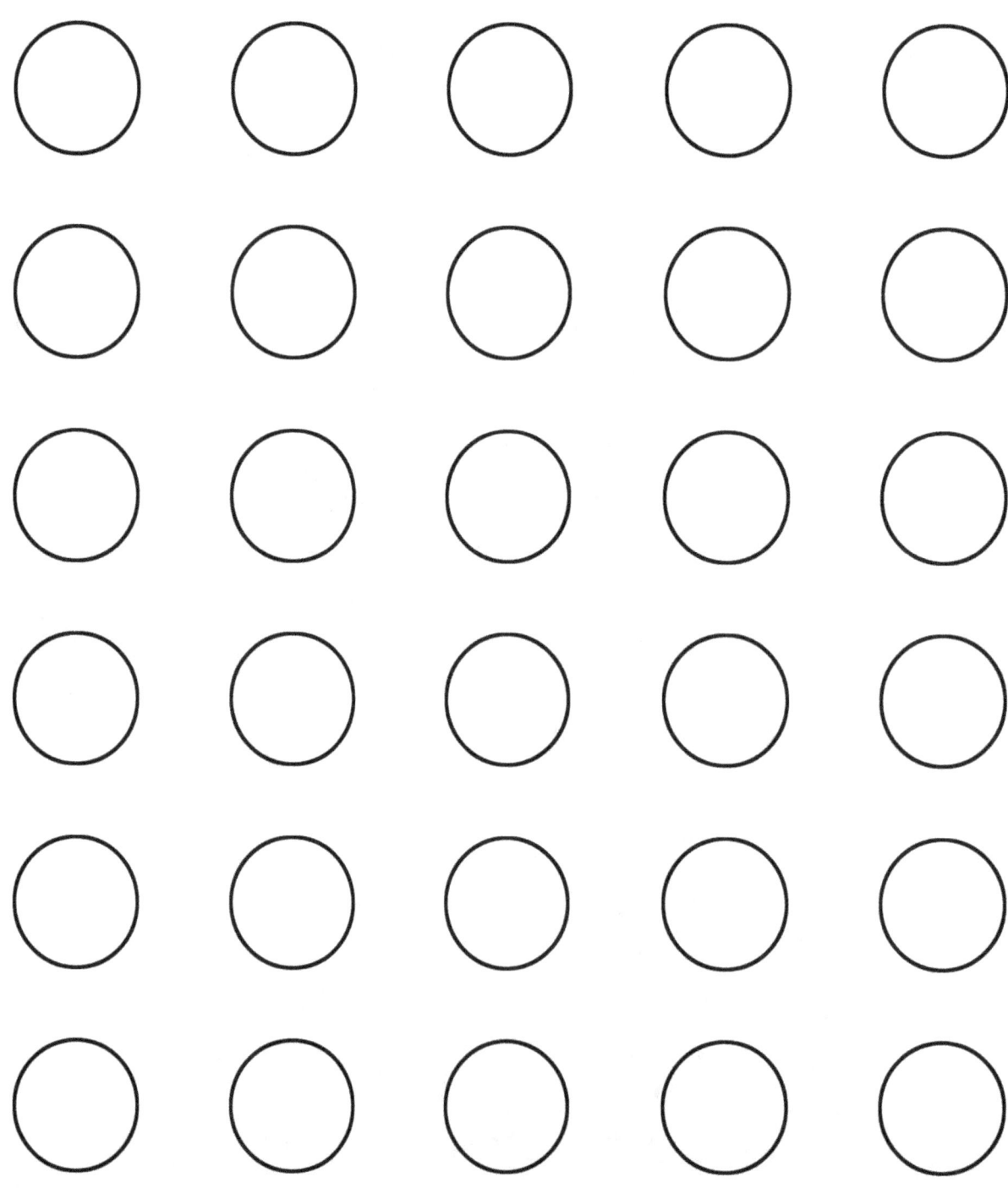

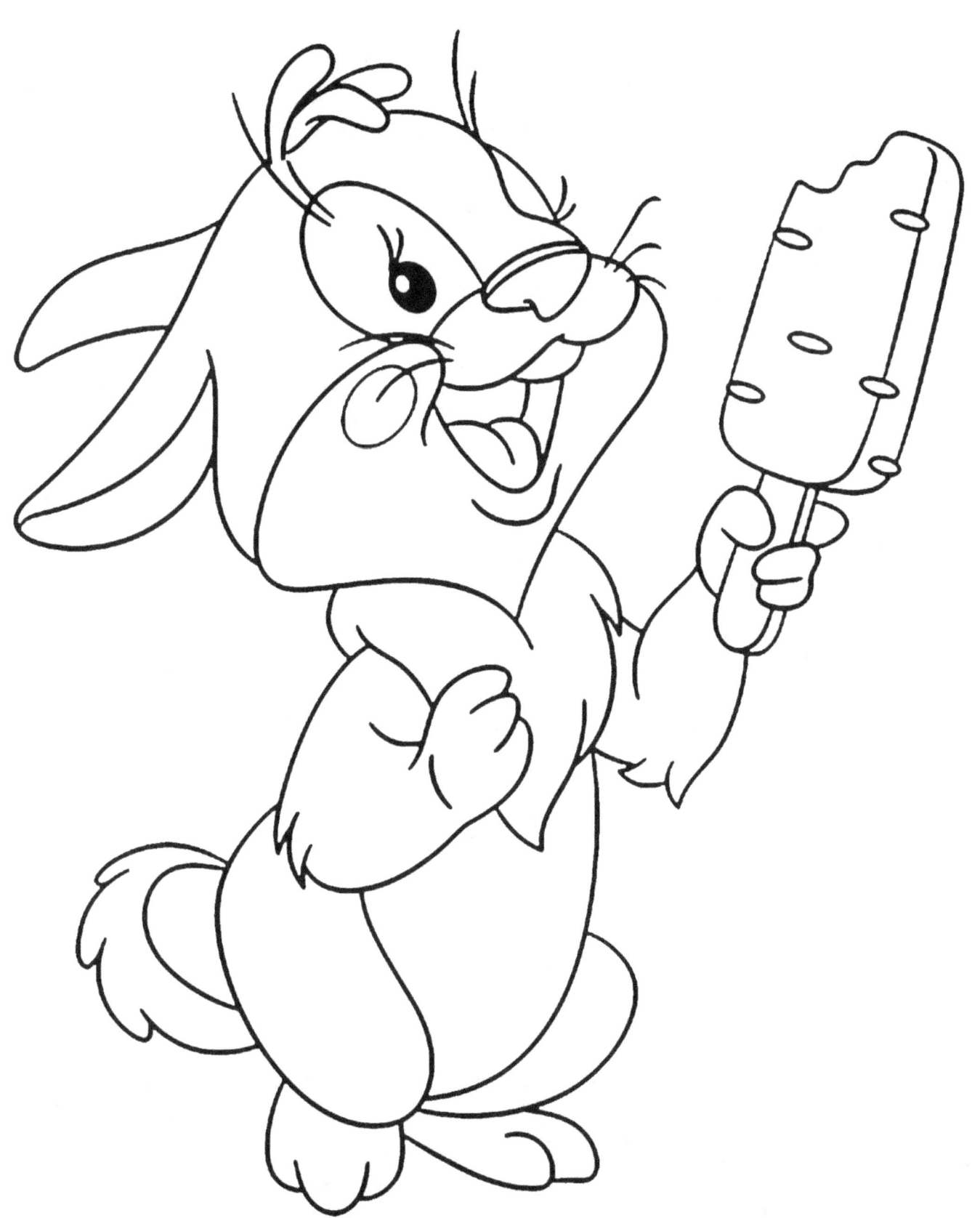

Test Your Color

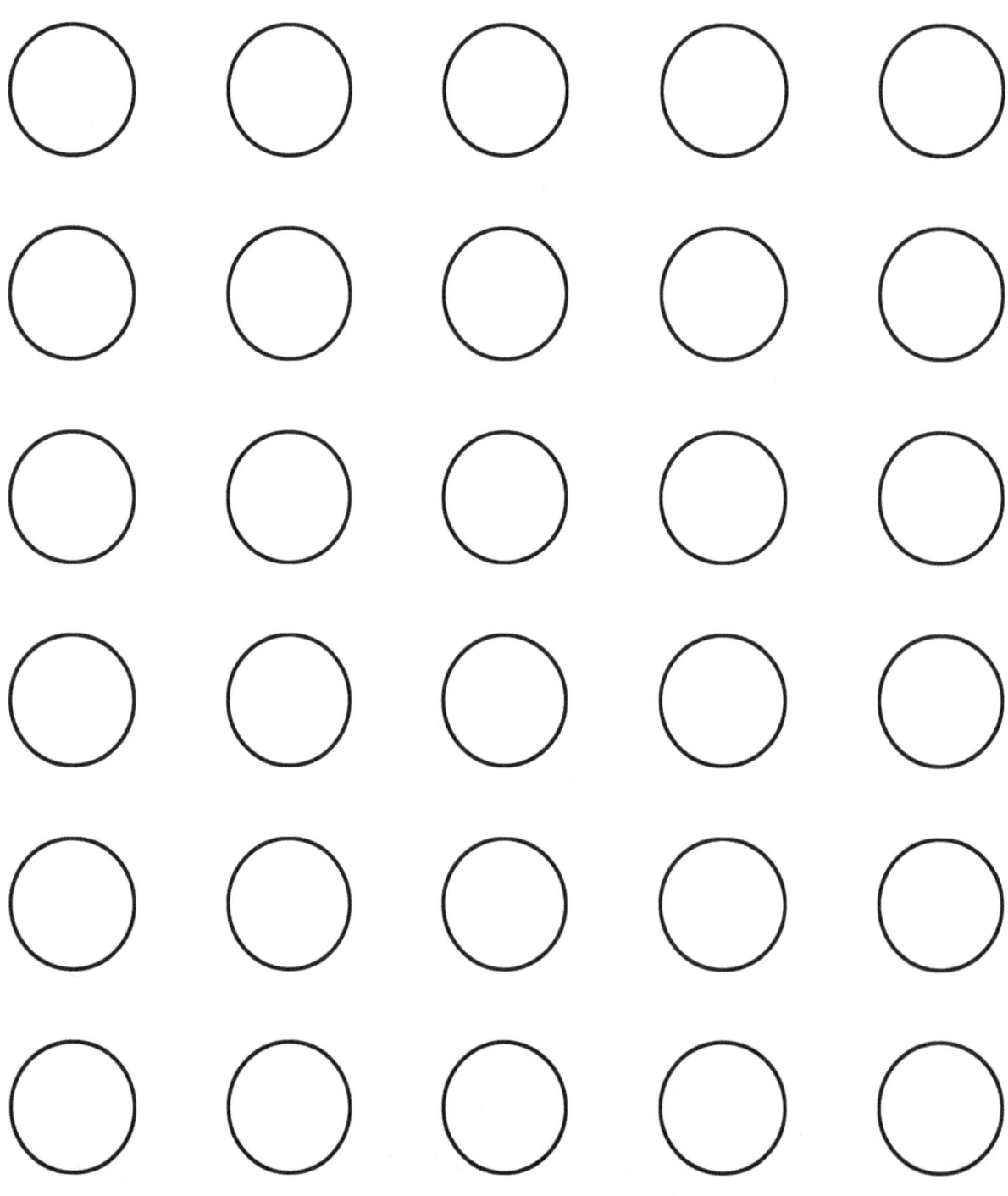

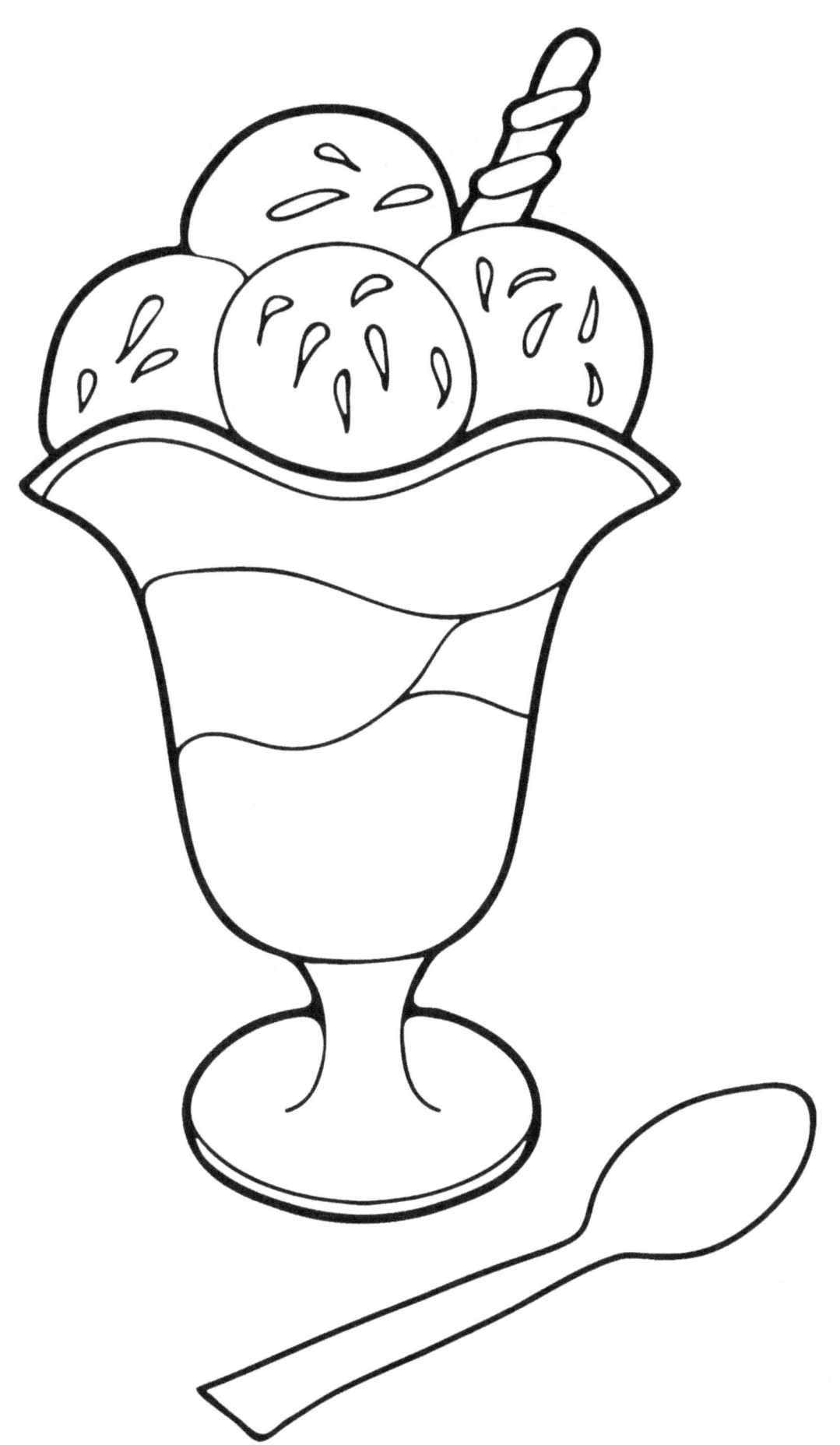

Test Your Color

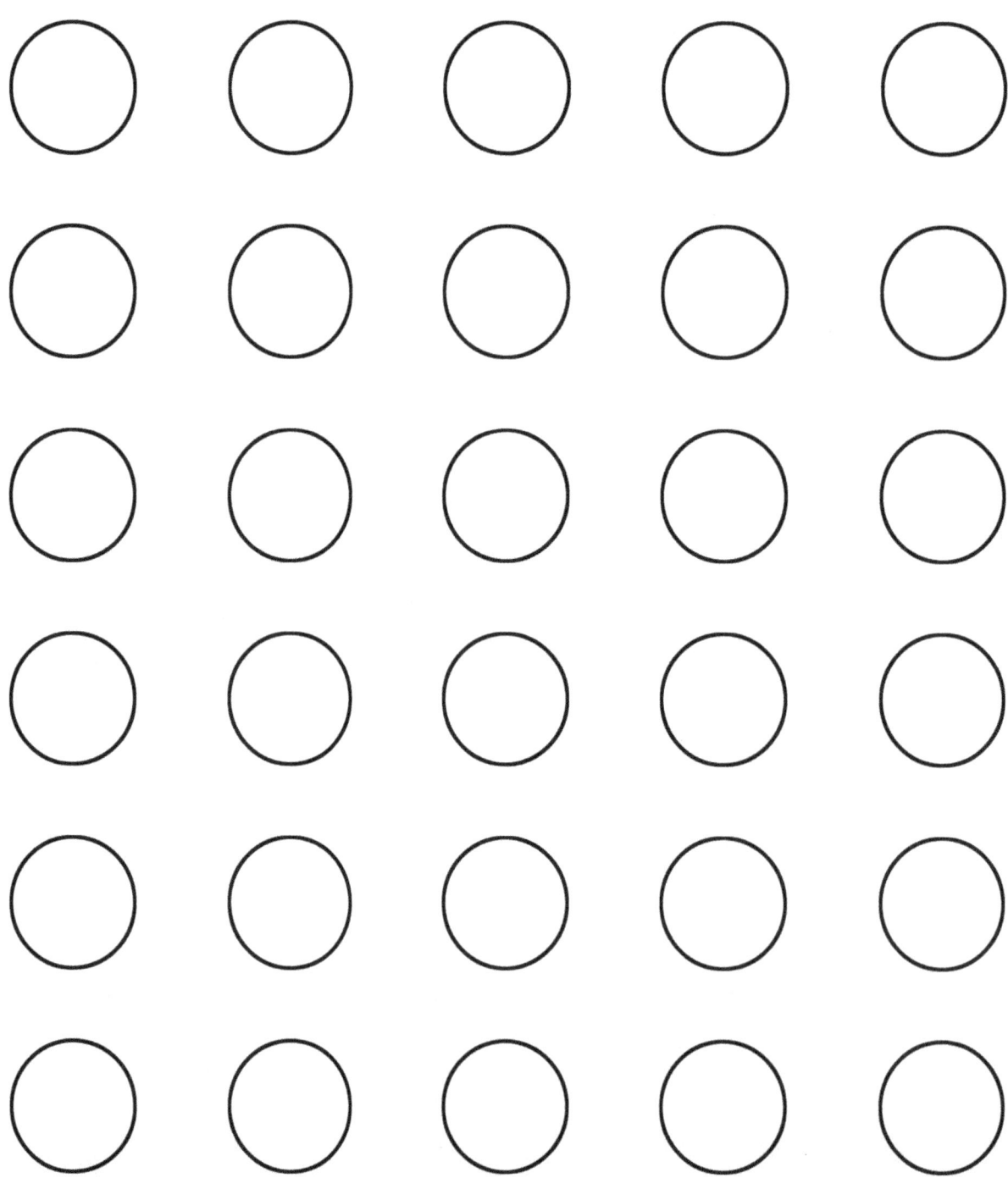

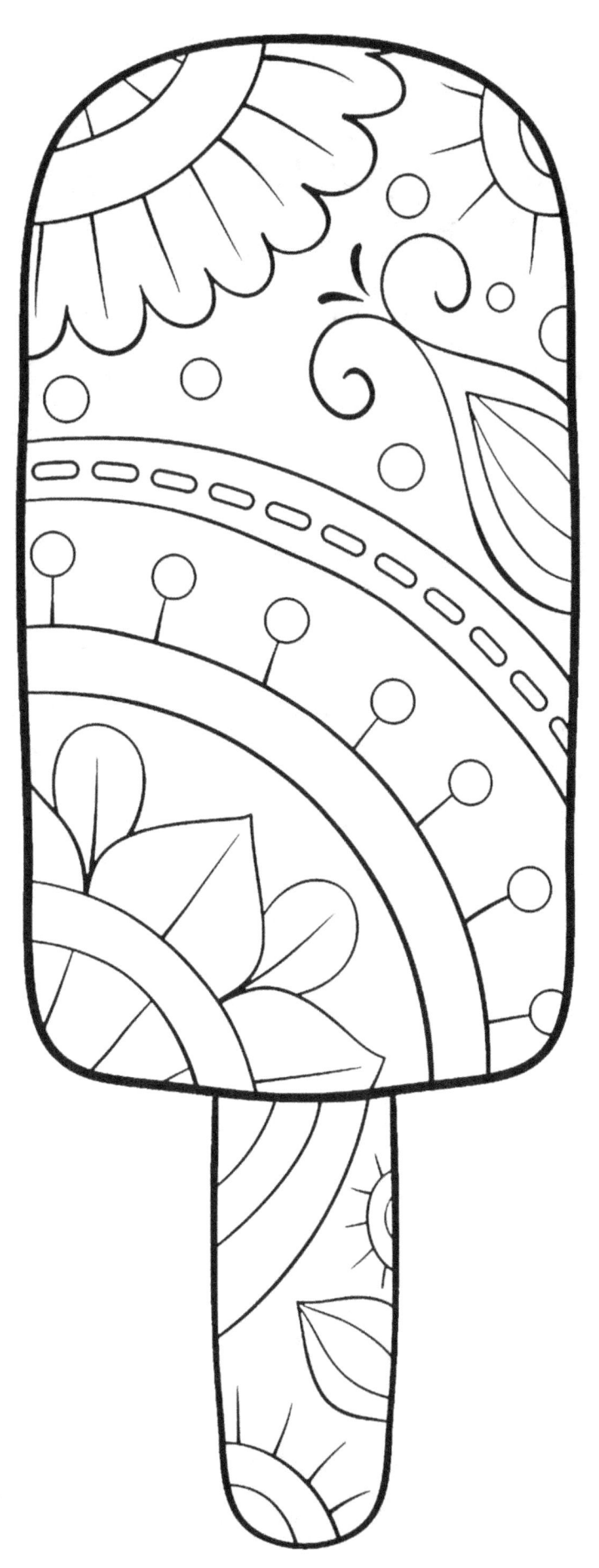

Test Your Color

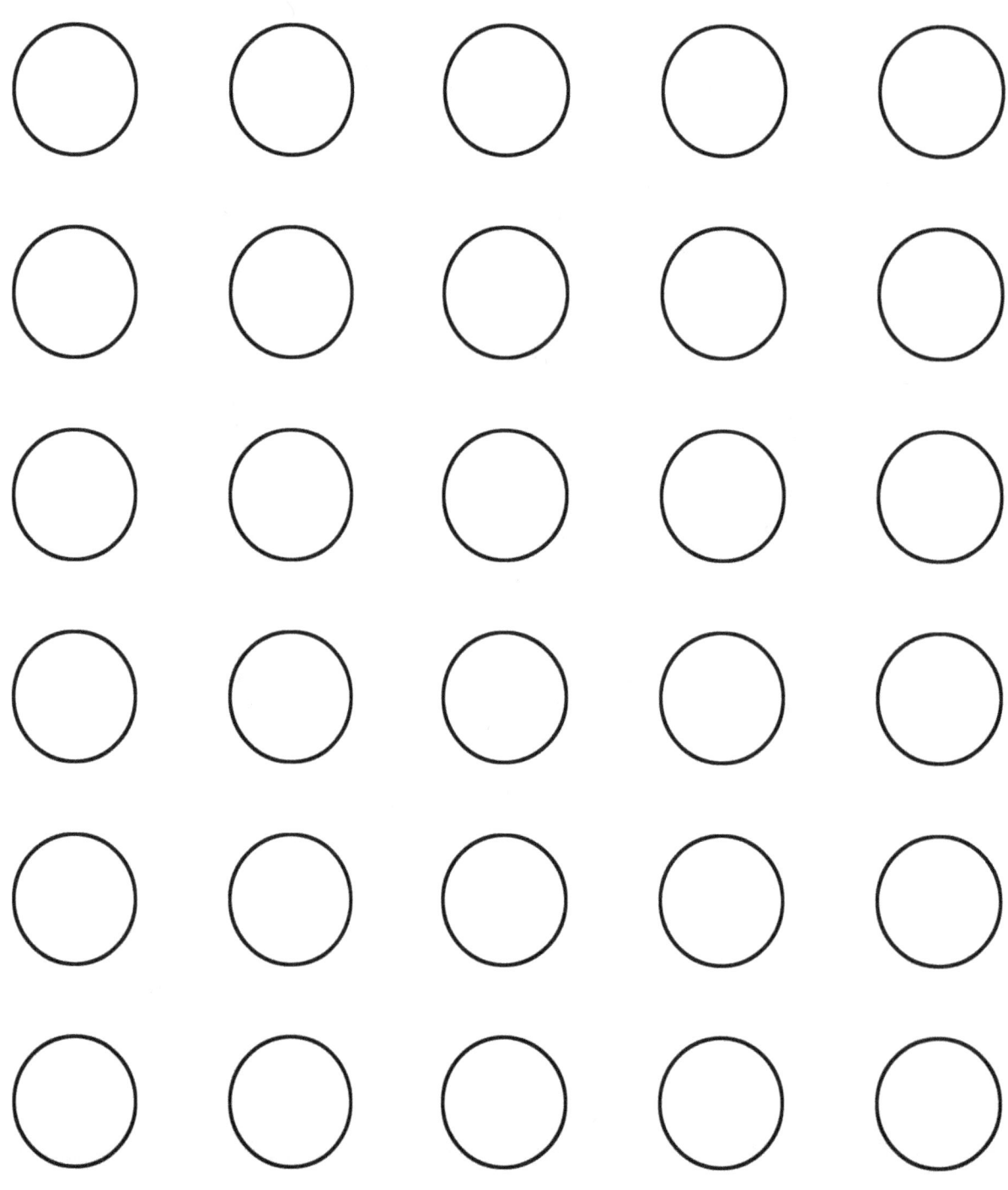

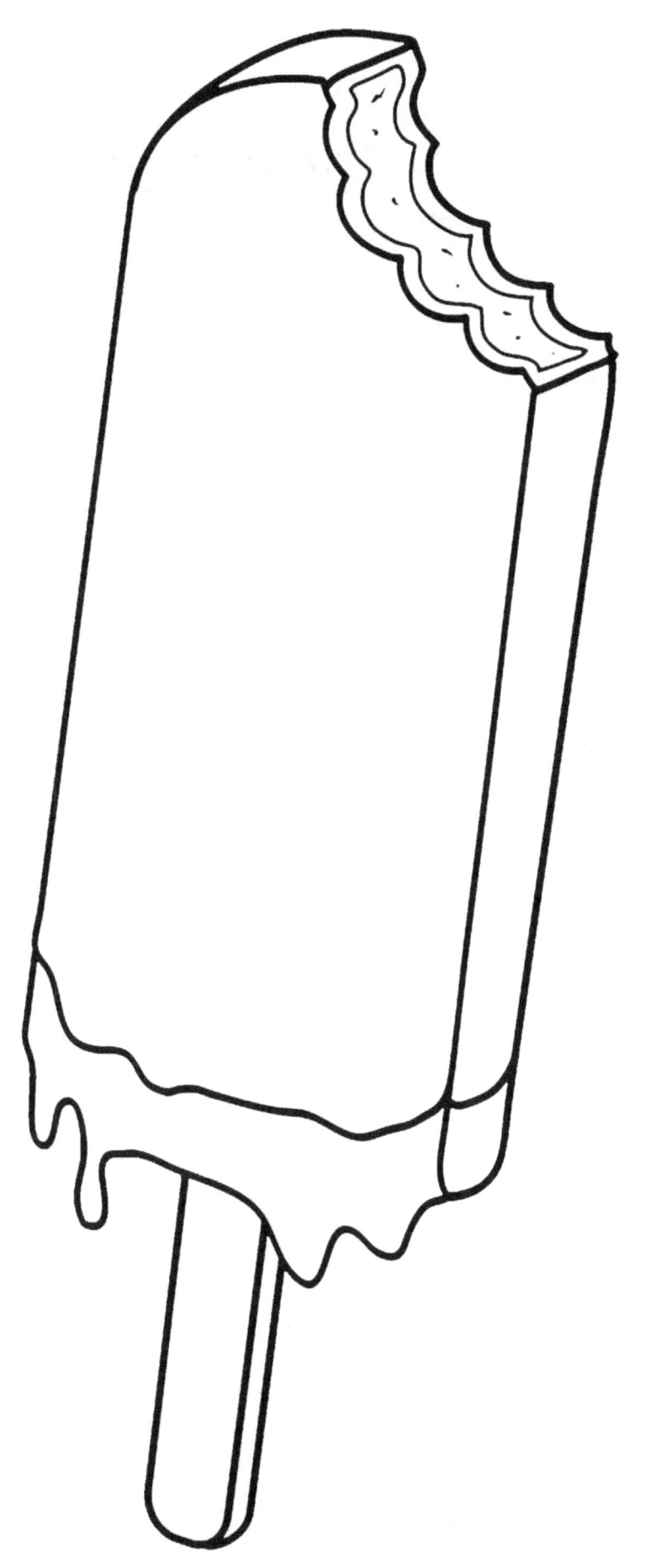

Test Your Color

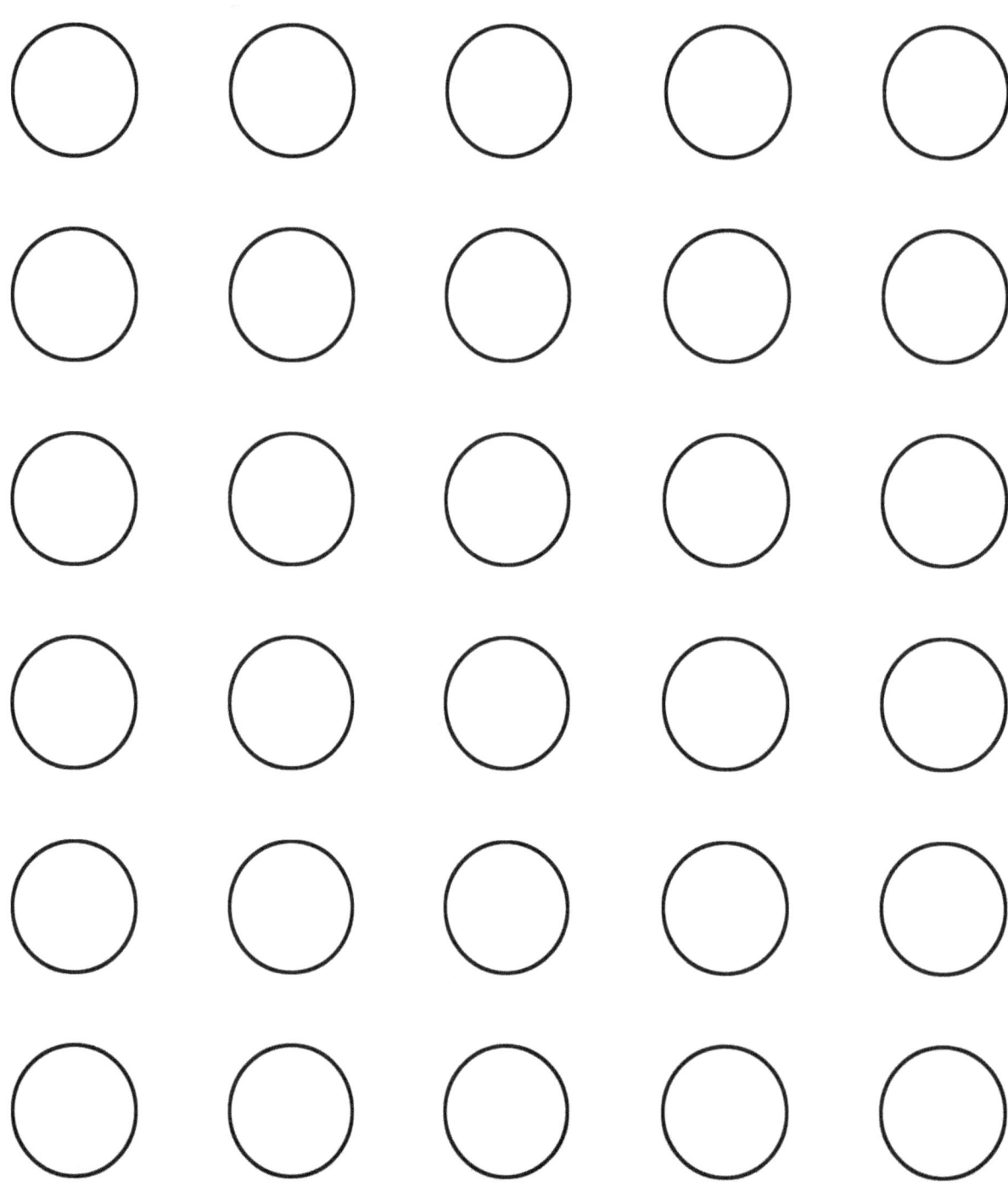

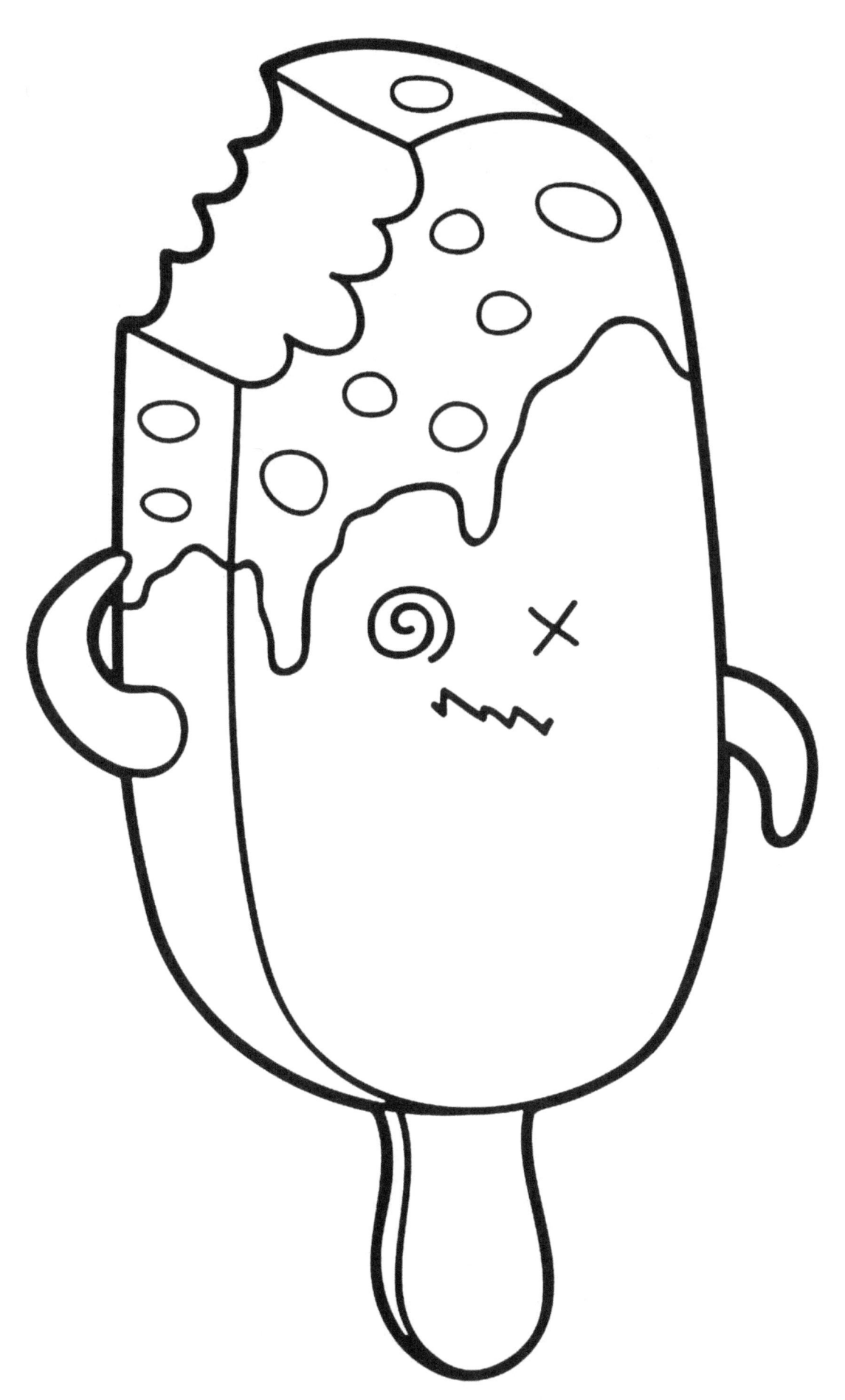

Test Your Color

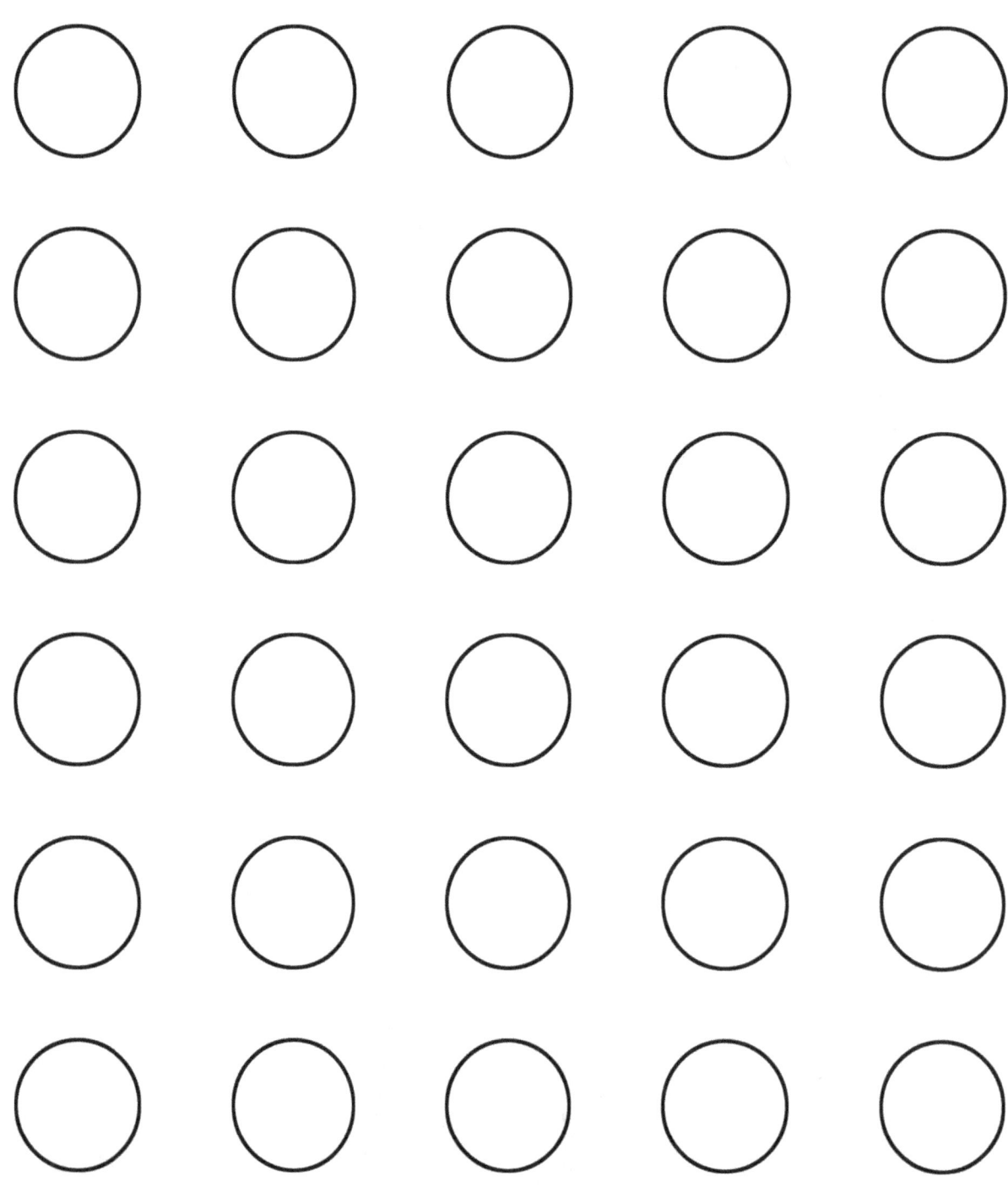

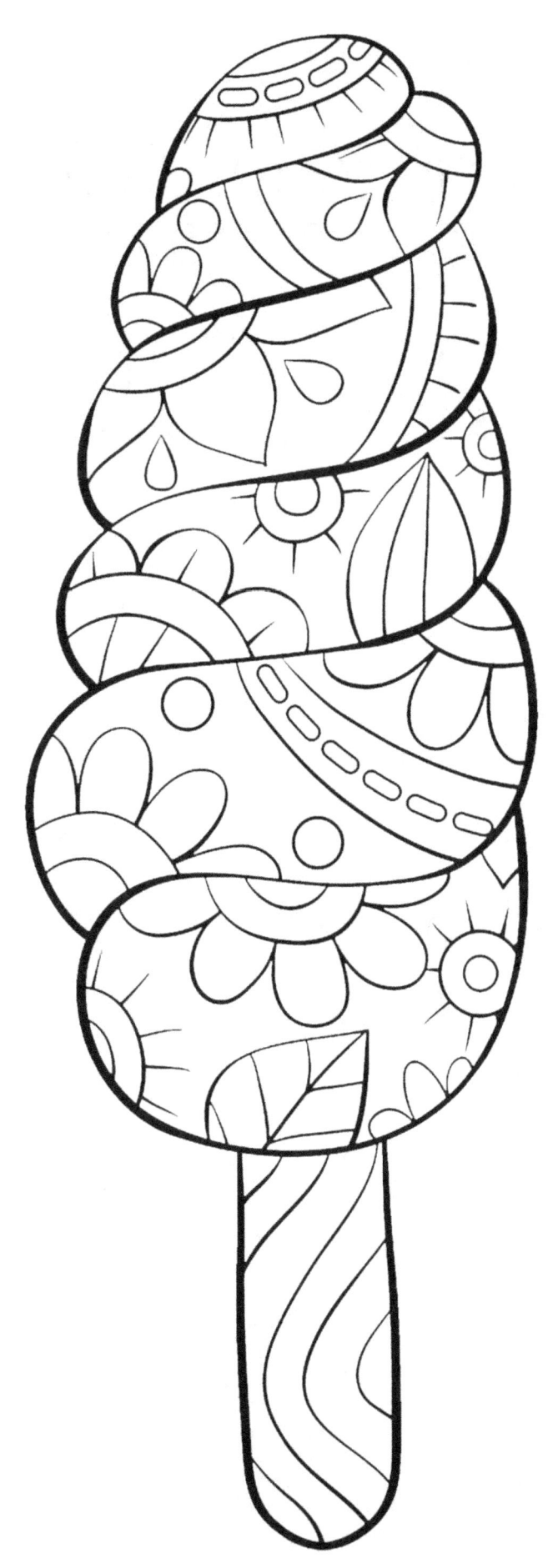

Test Your Color

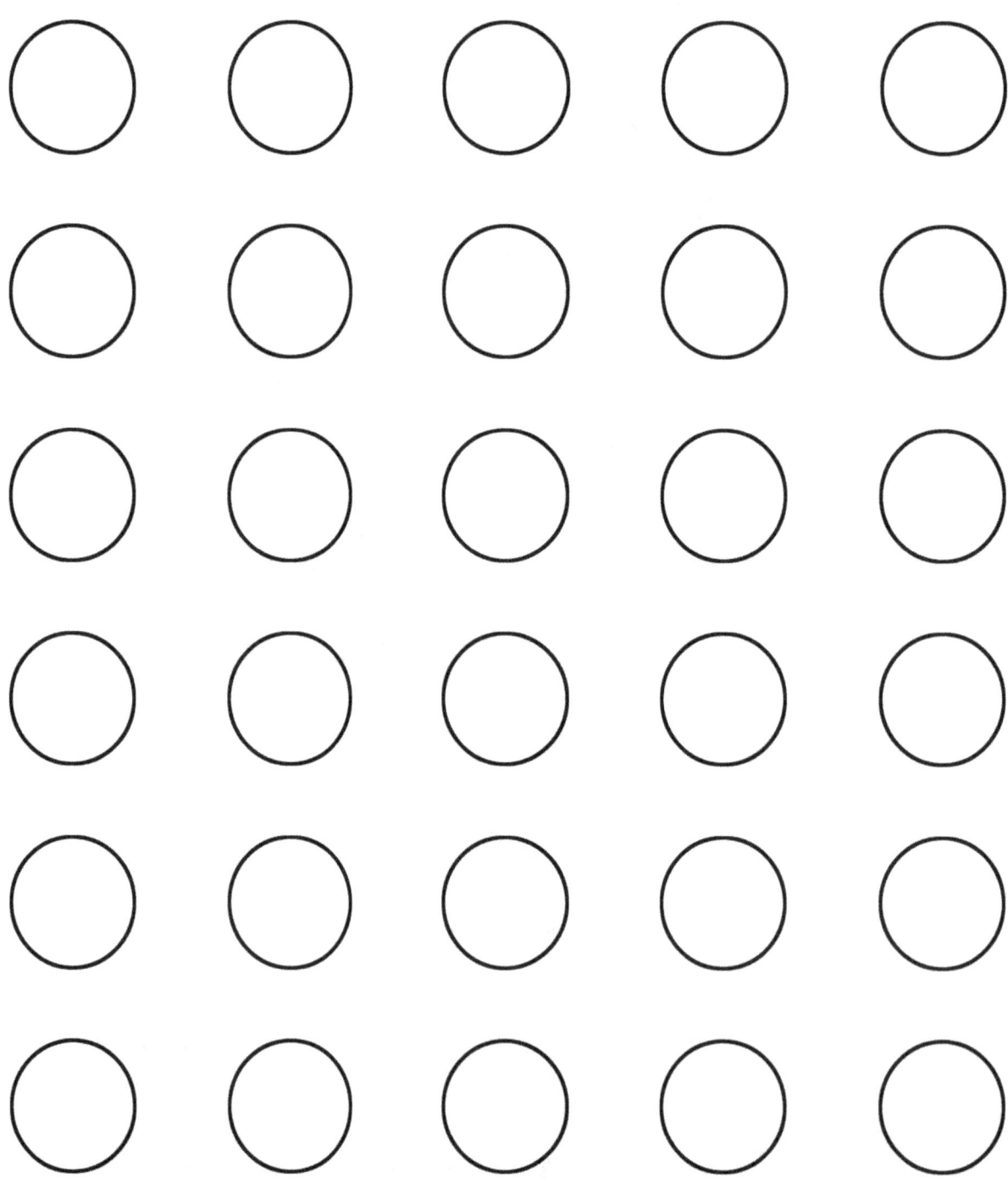

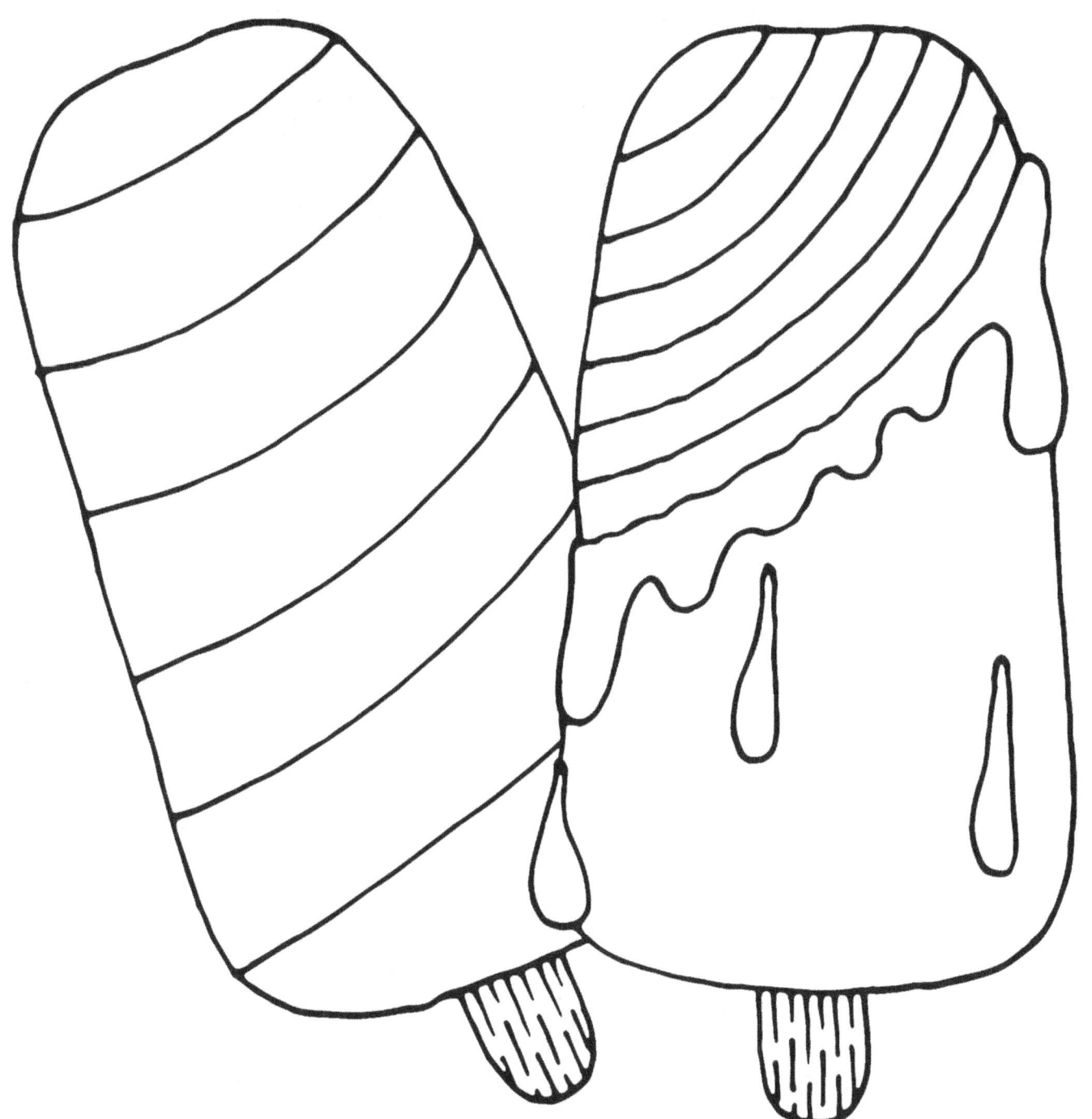

Test Your Color

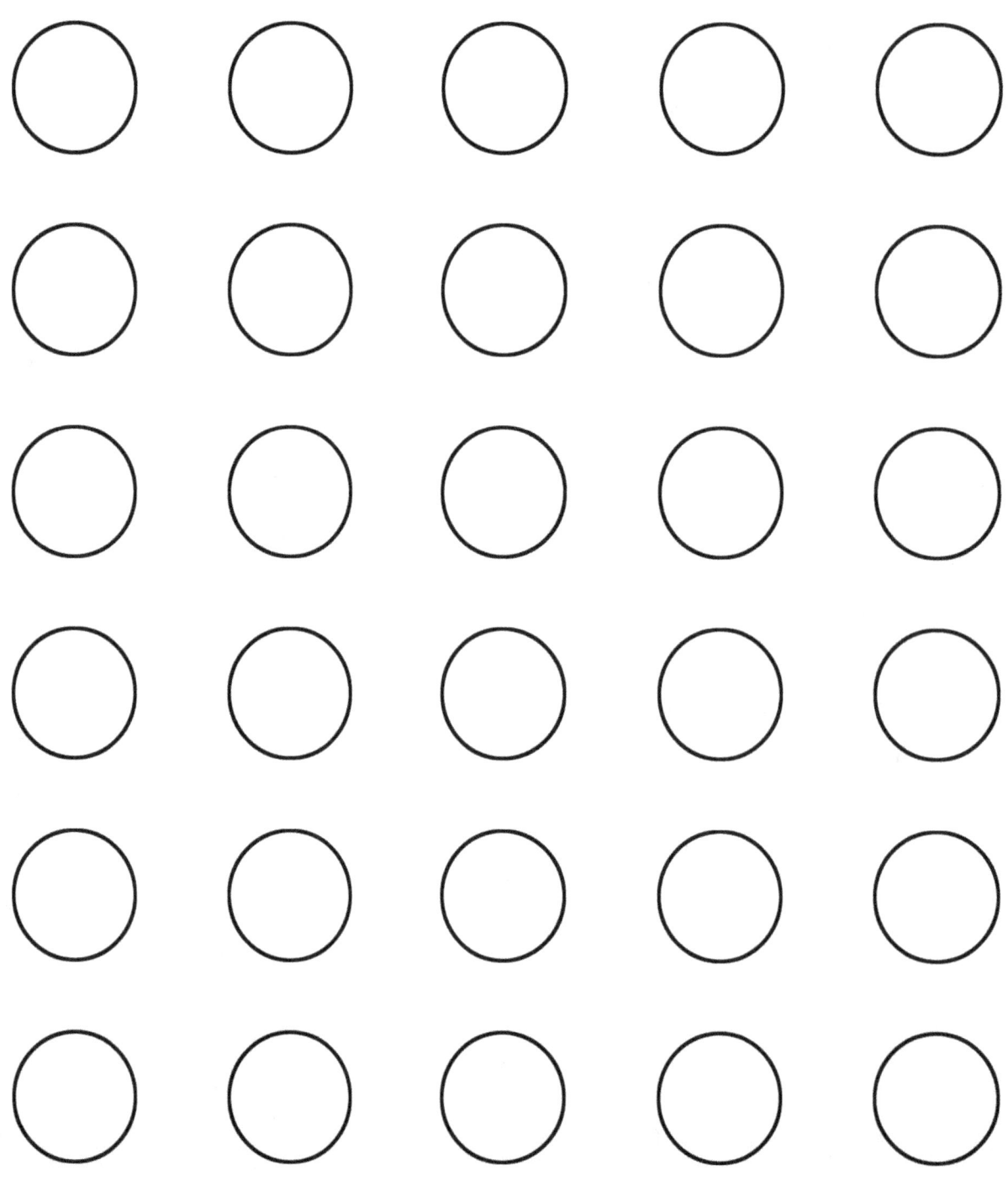

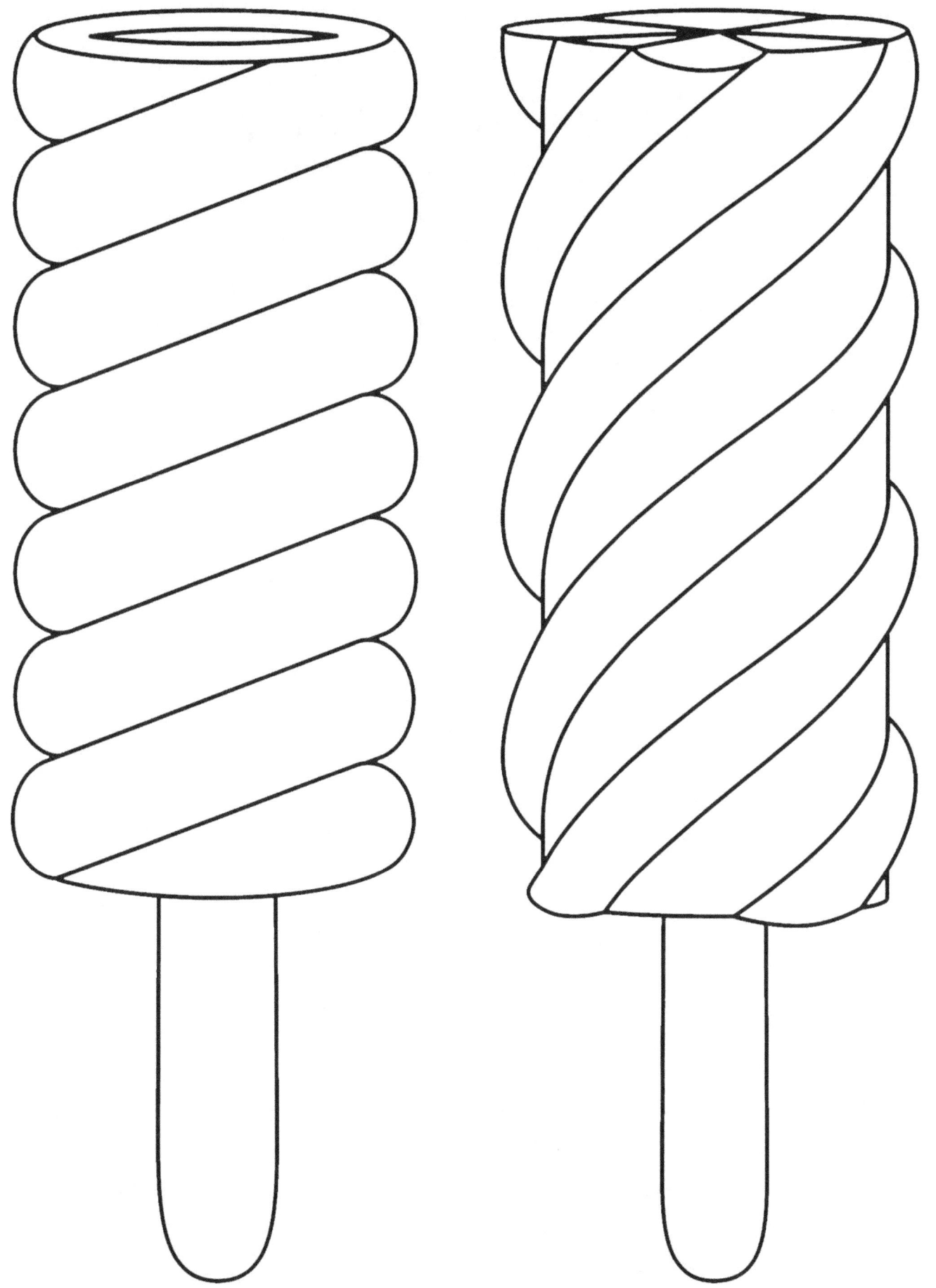

Test Your Color

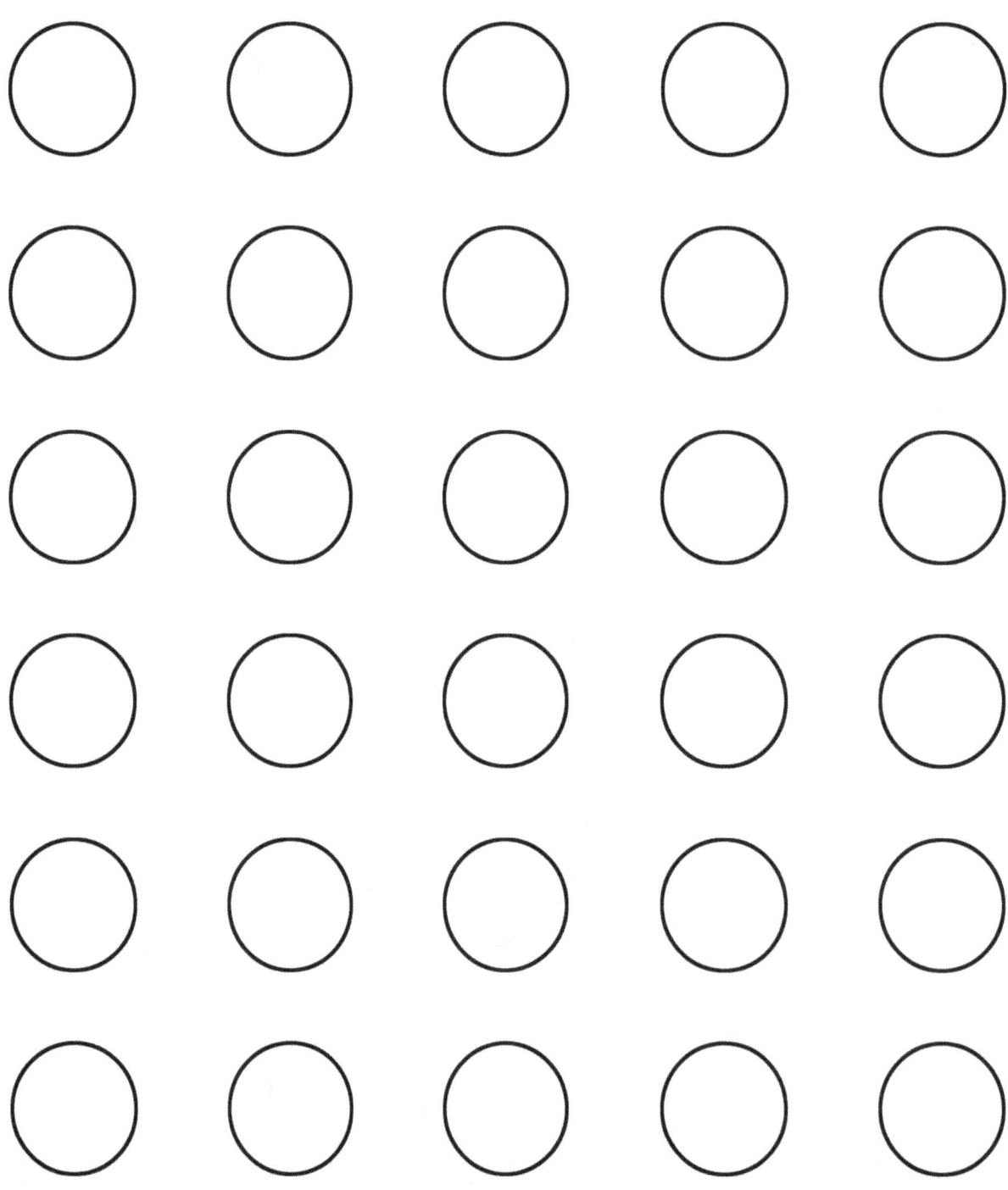

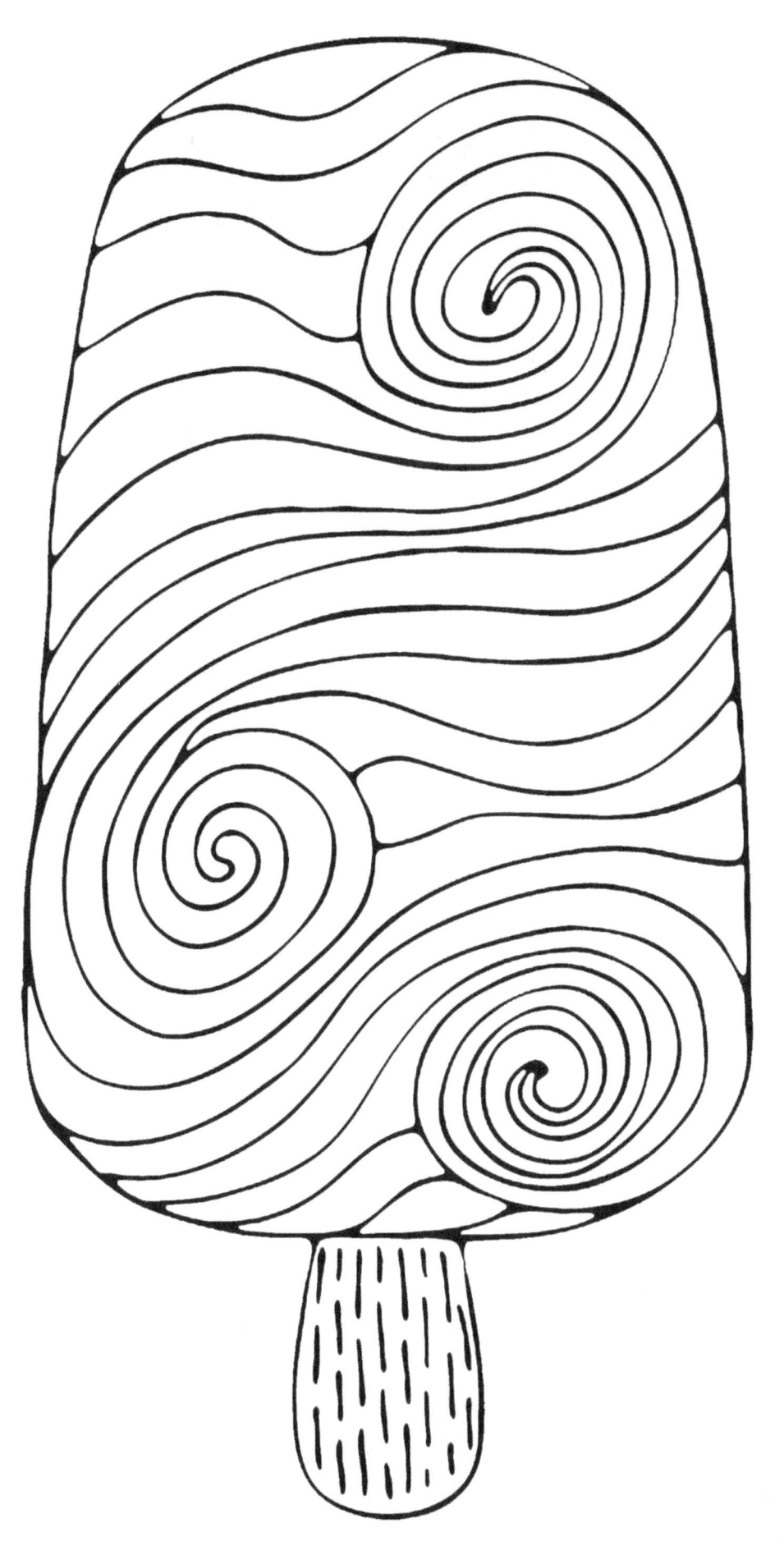

Test Your Color

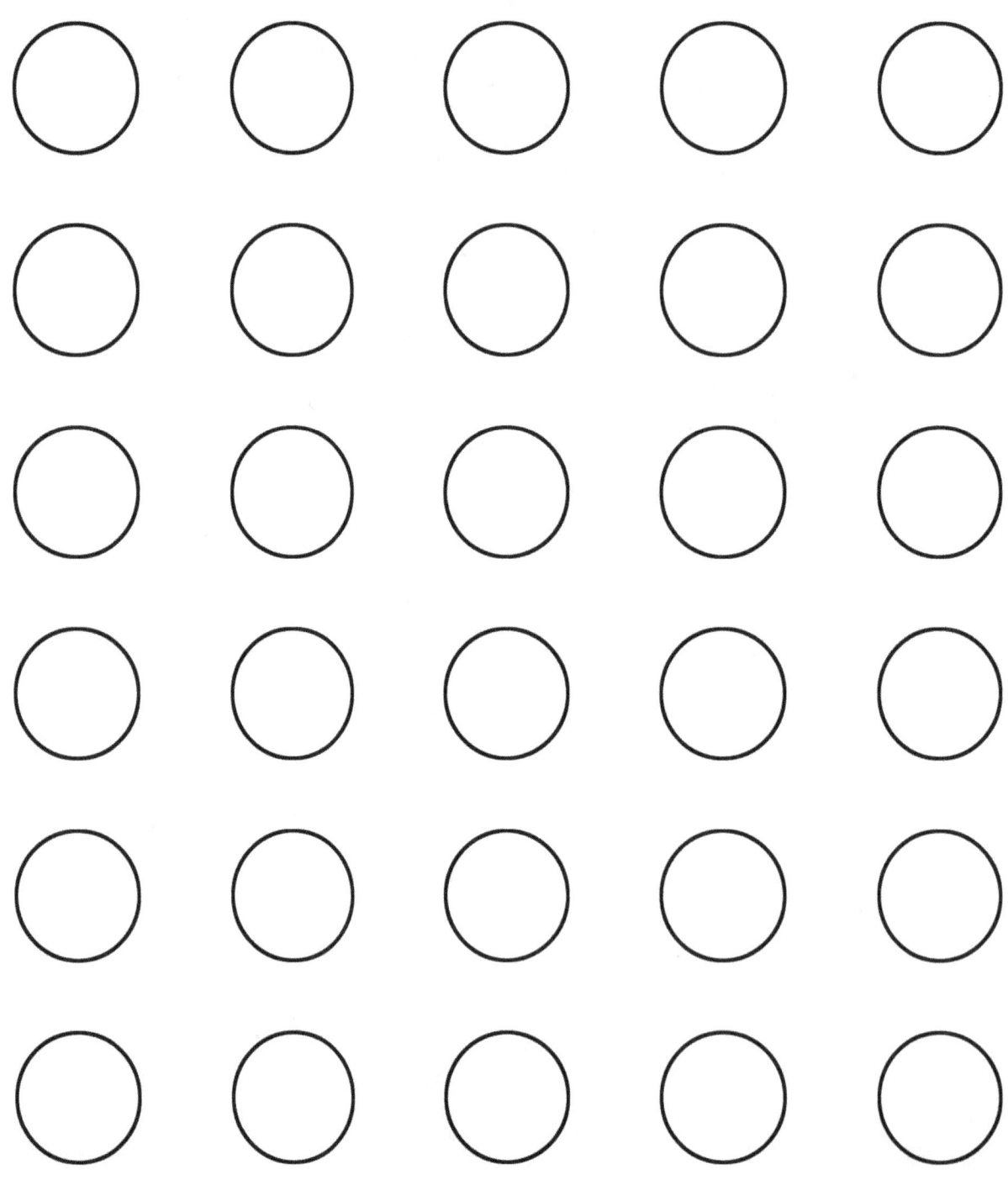

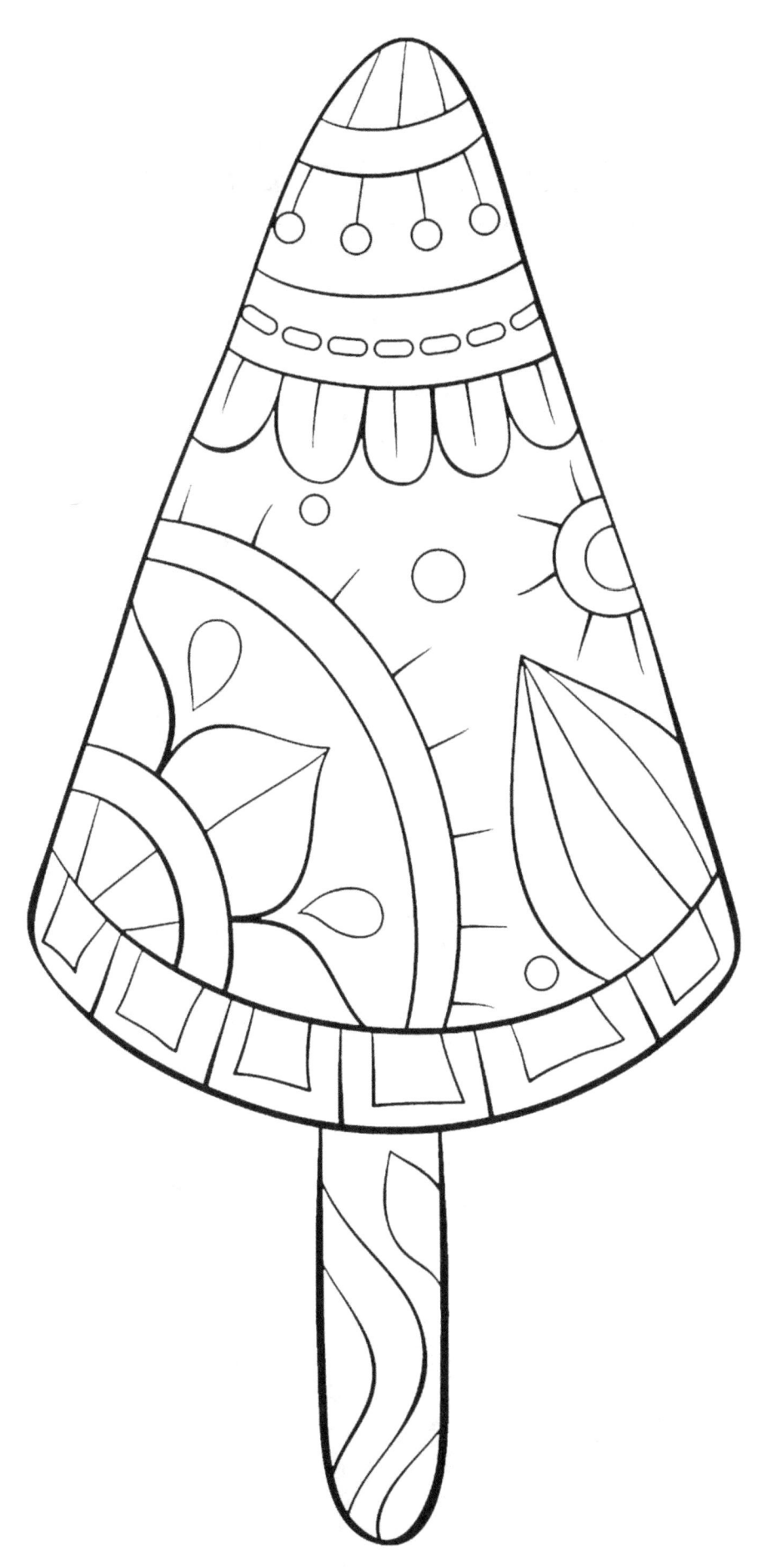

Test Your Color

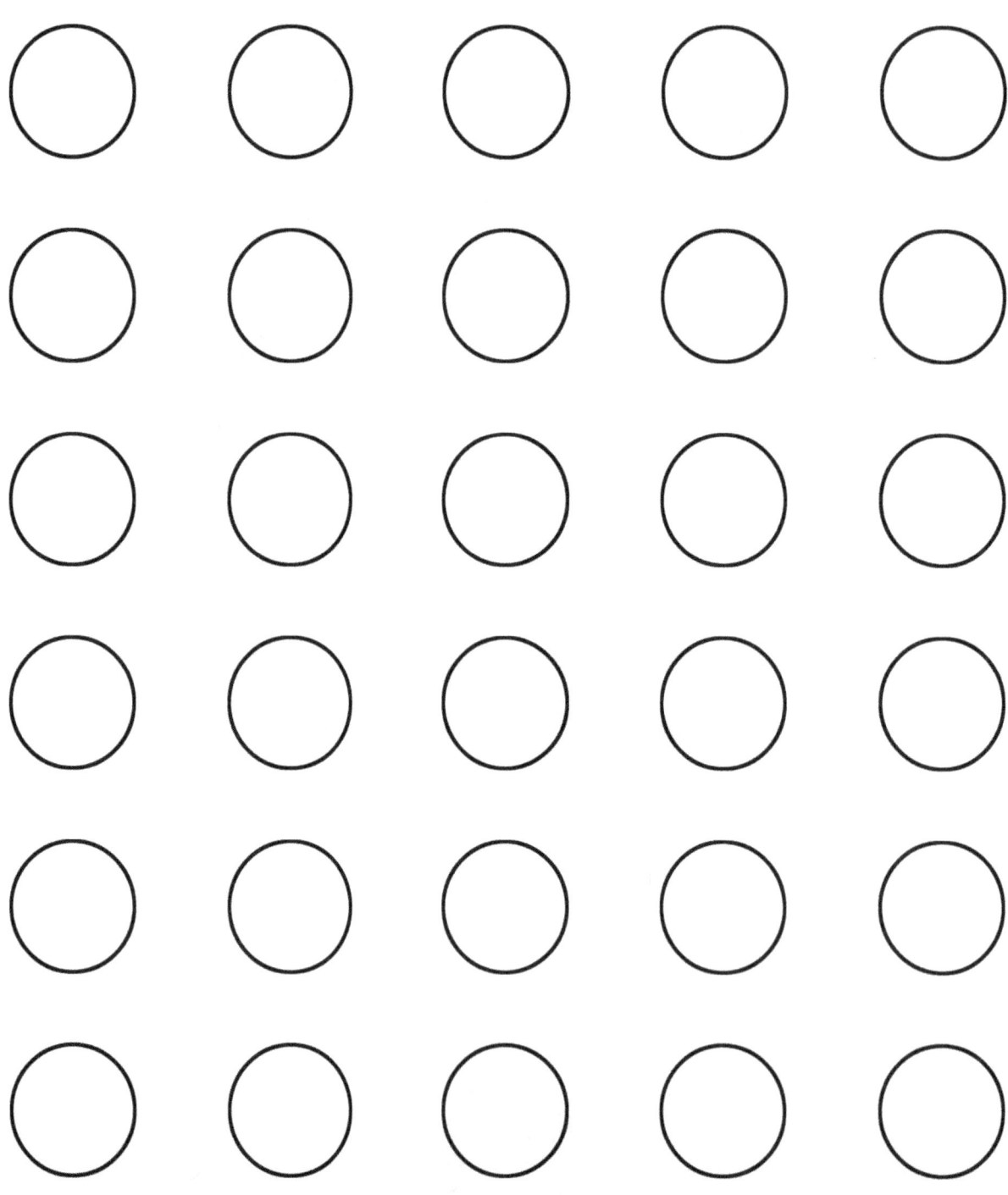

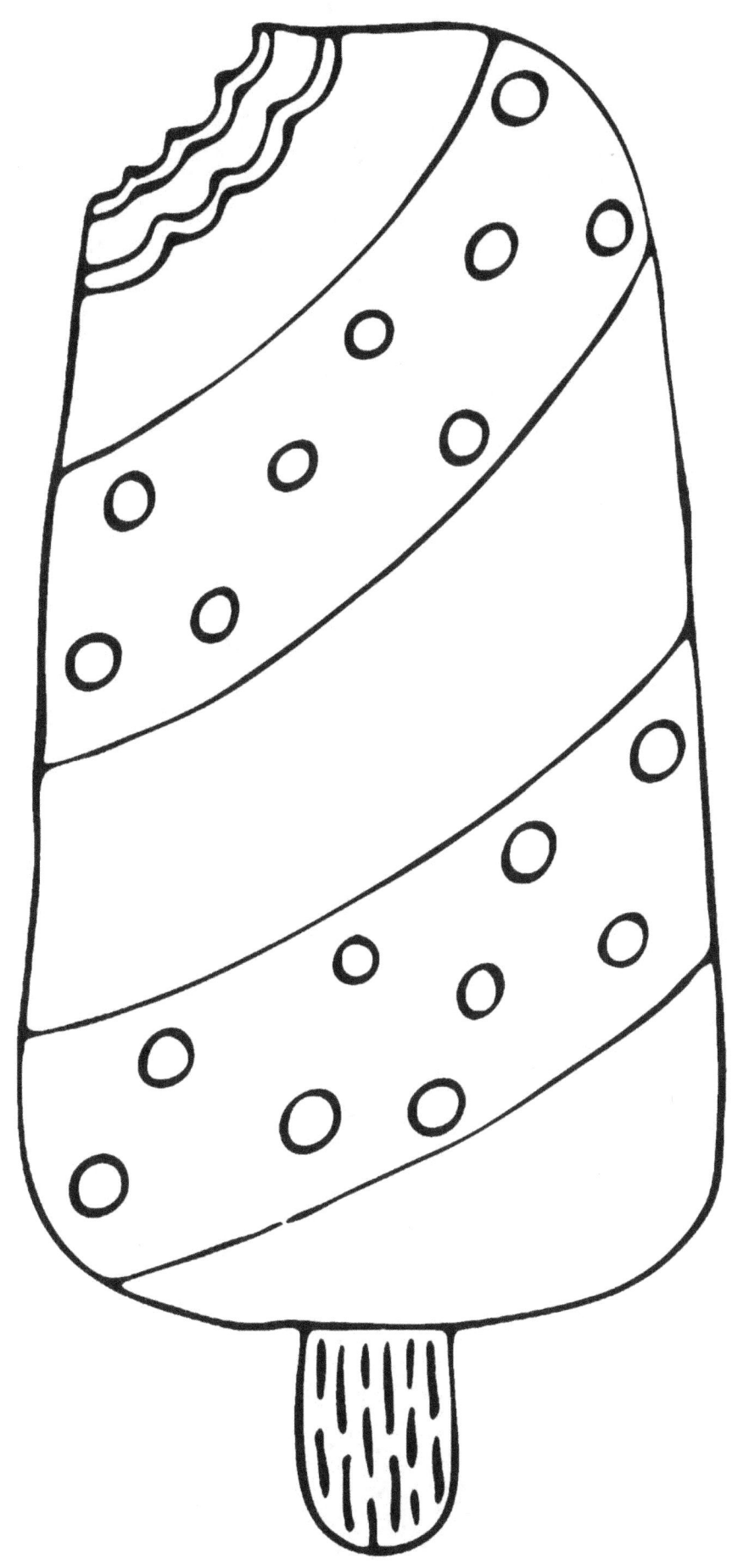

Test Your Color

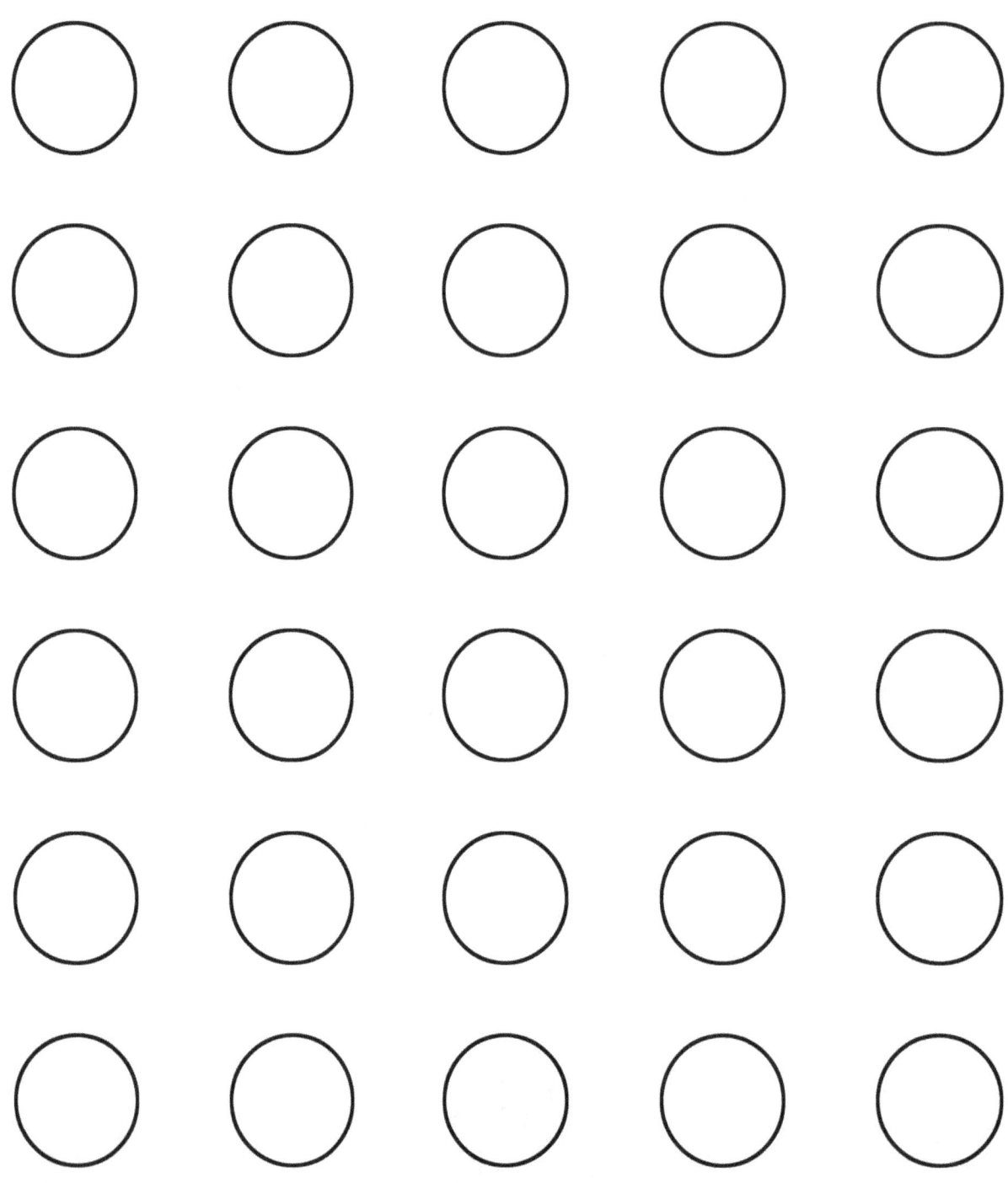

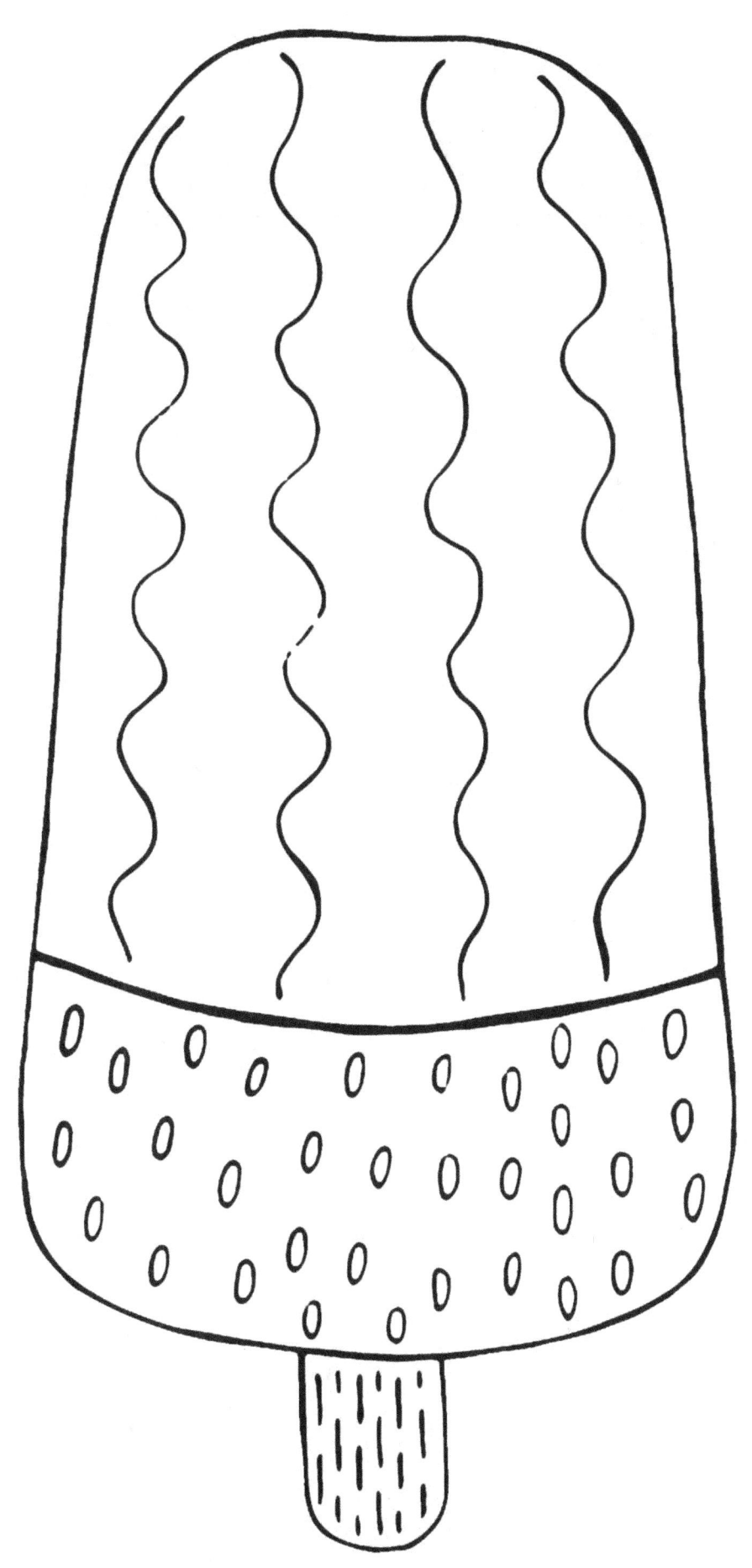

Test Your Color

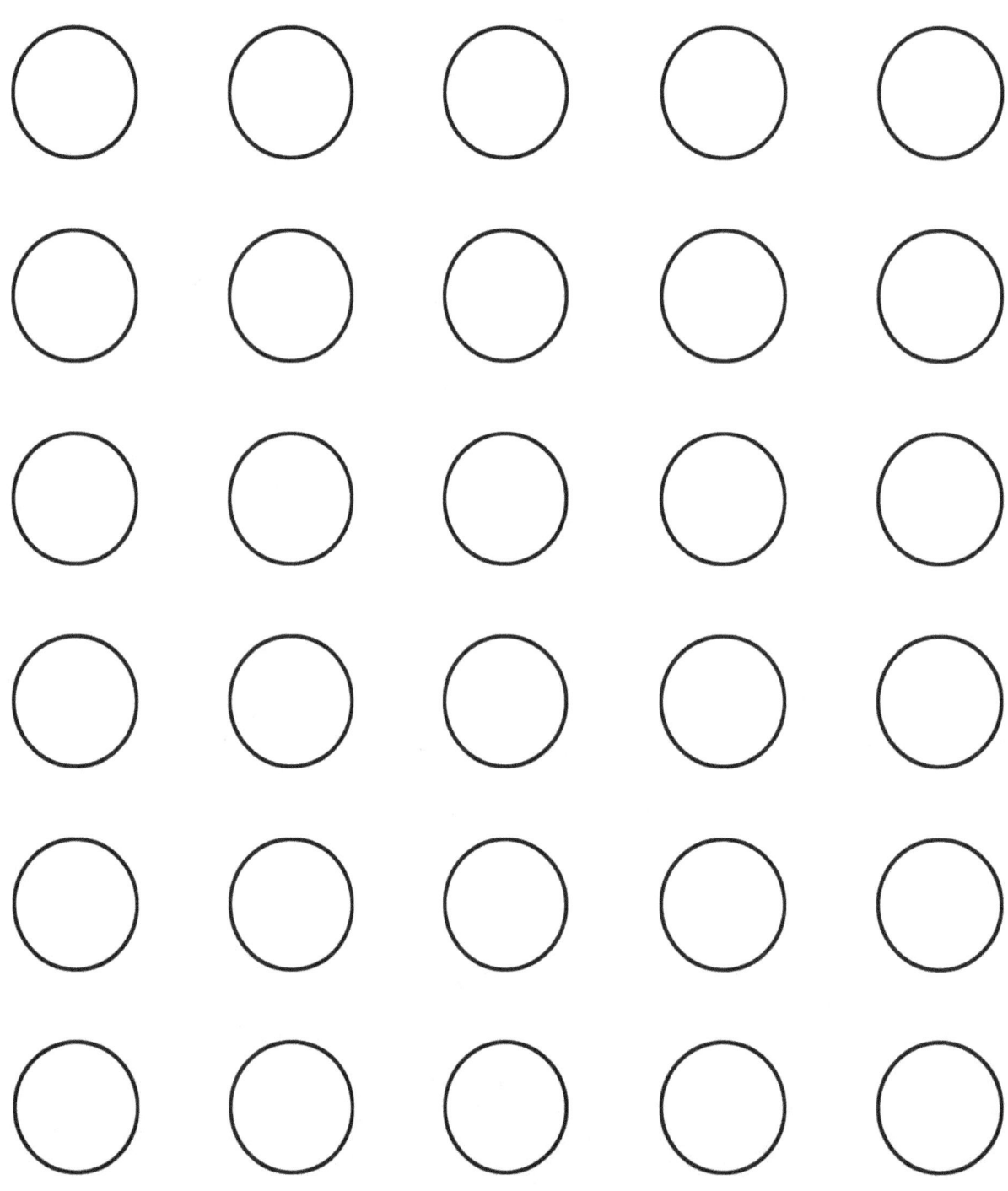

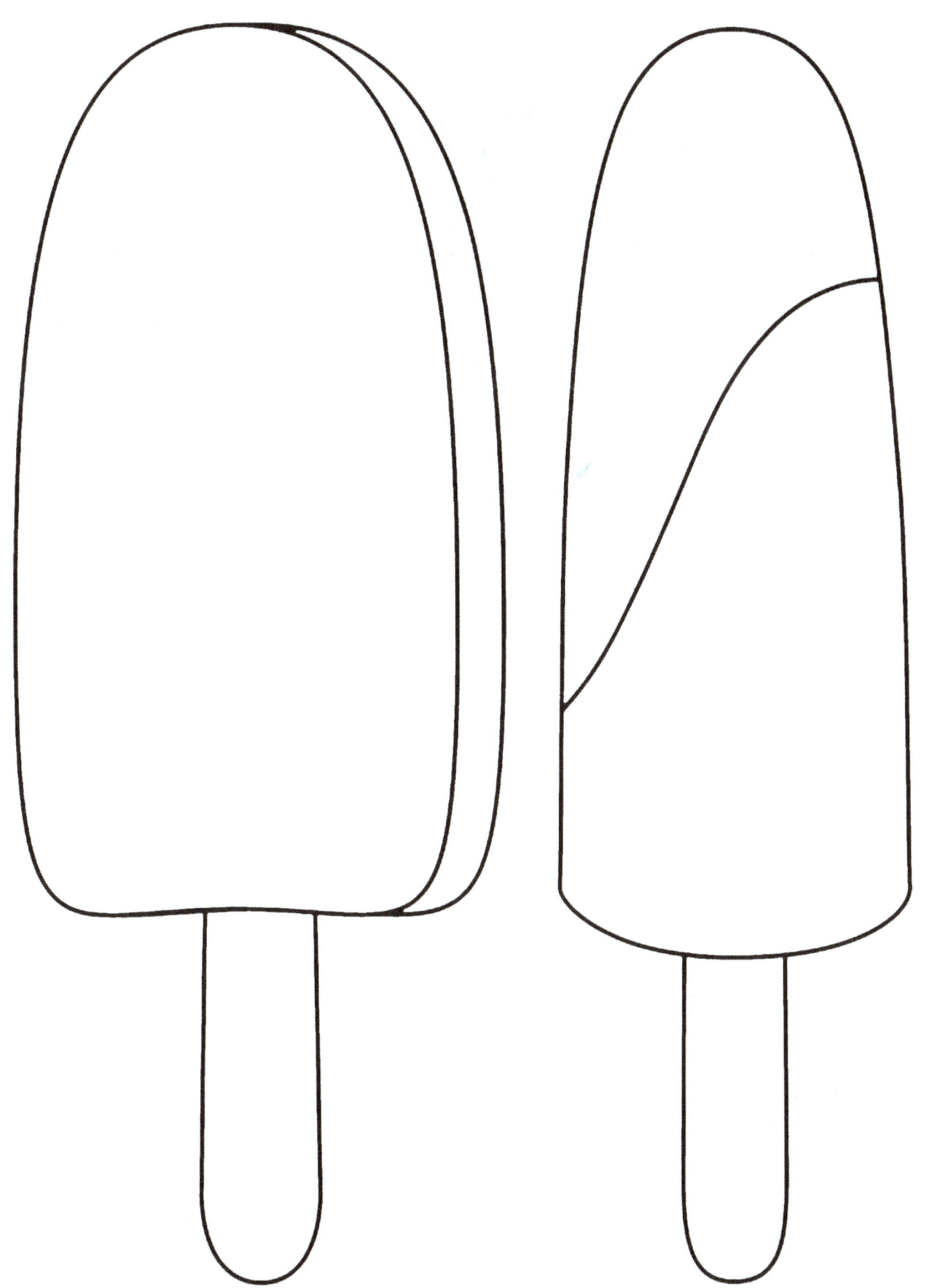

Test Your Color

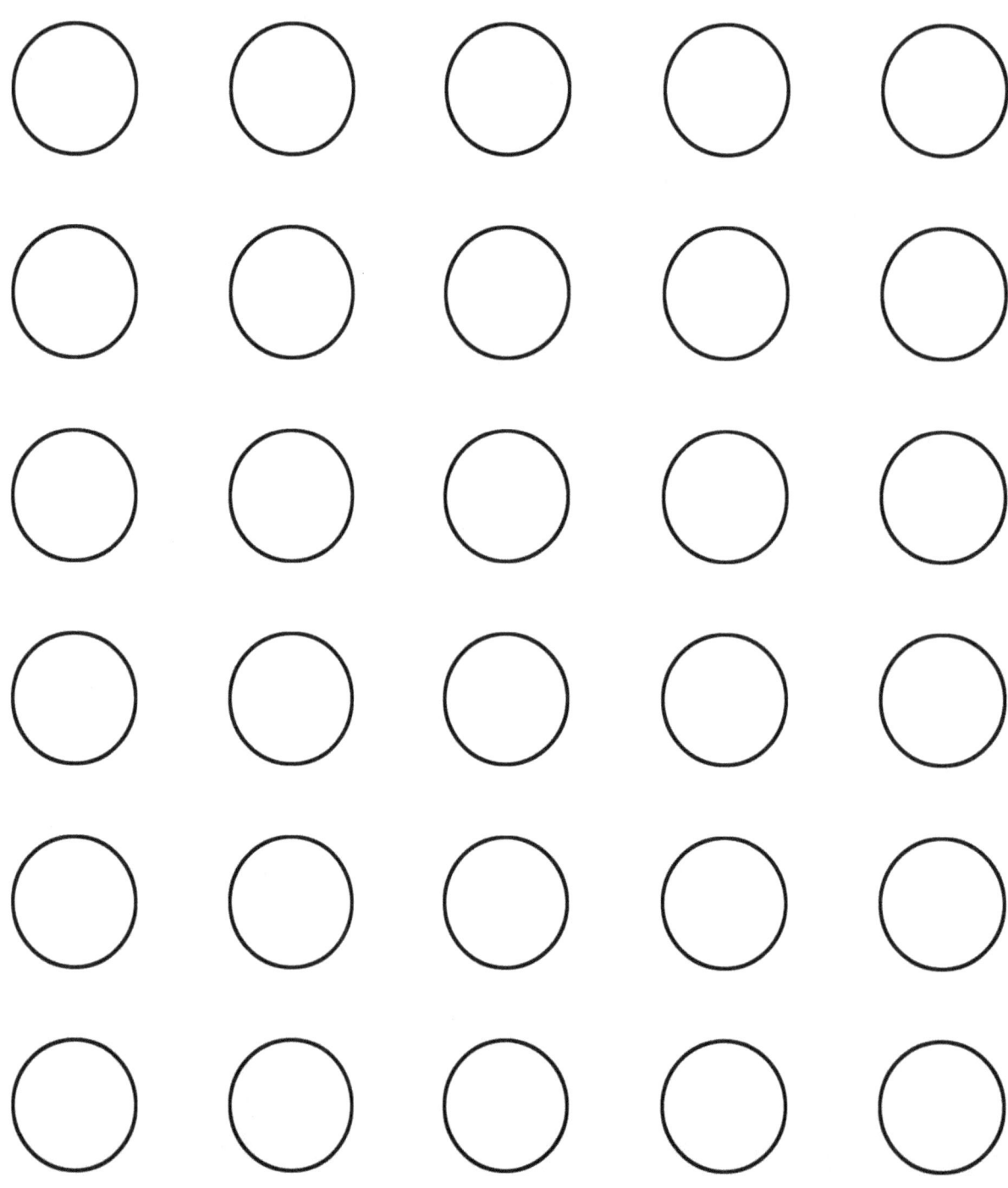

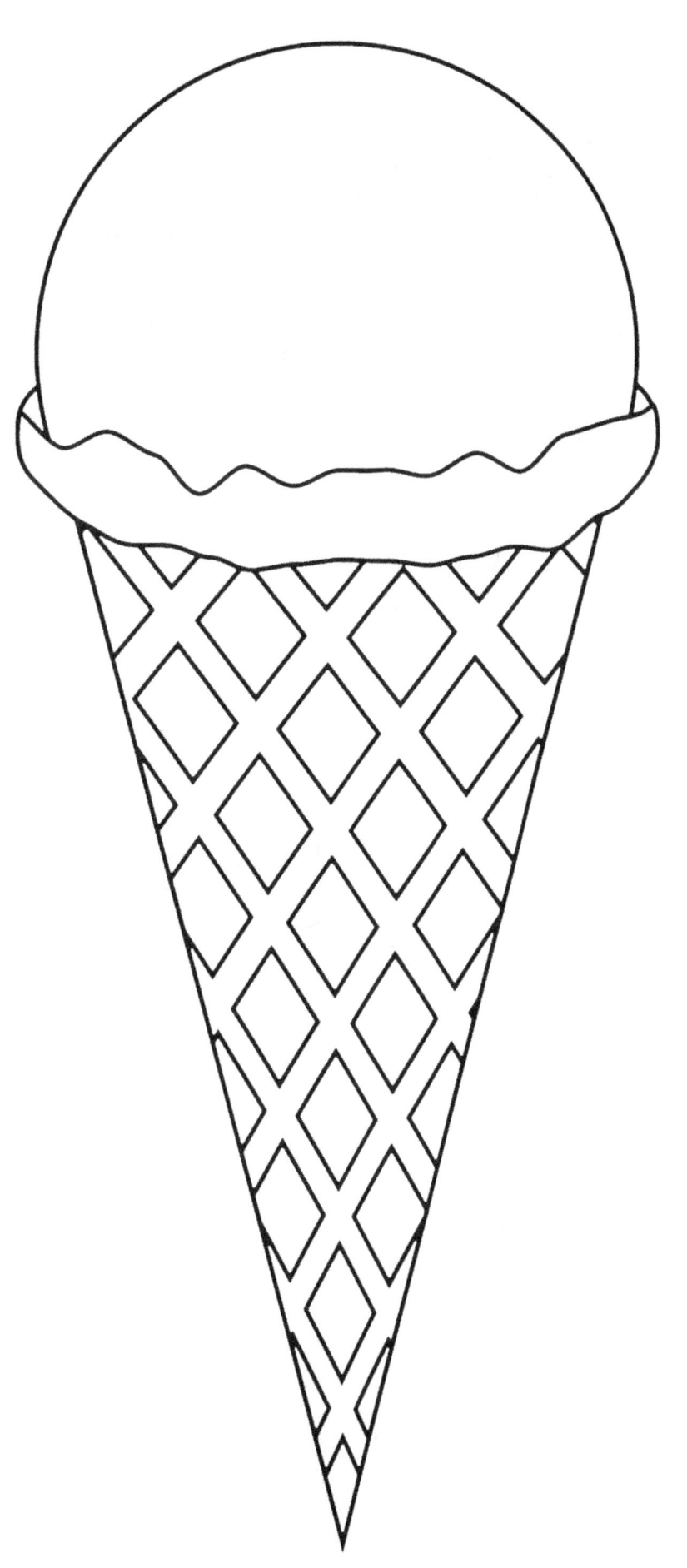

Test Your Color

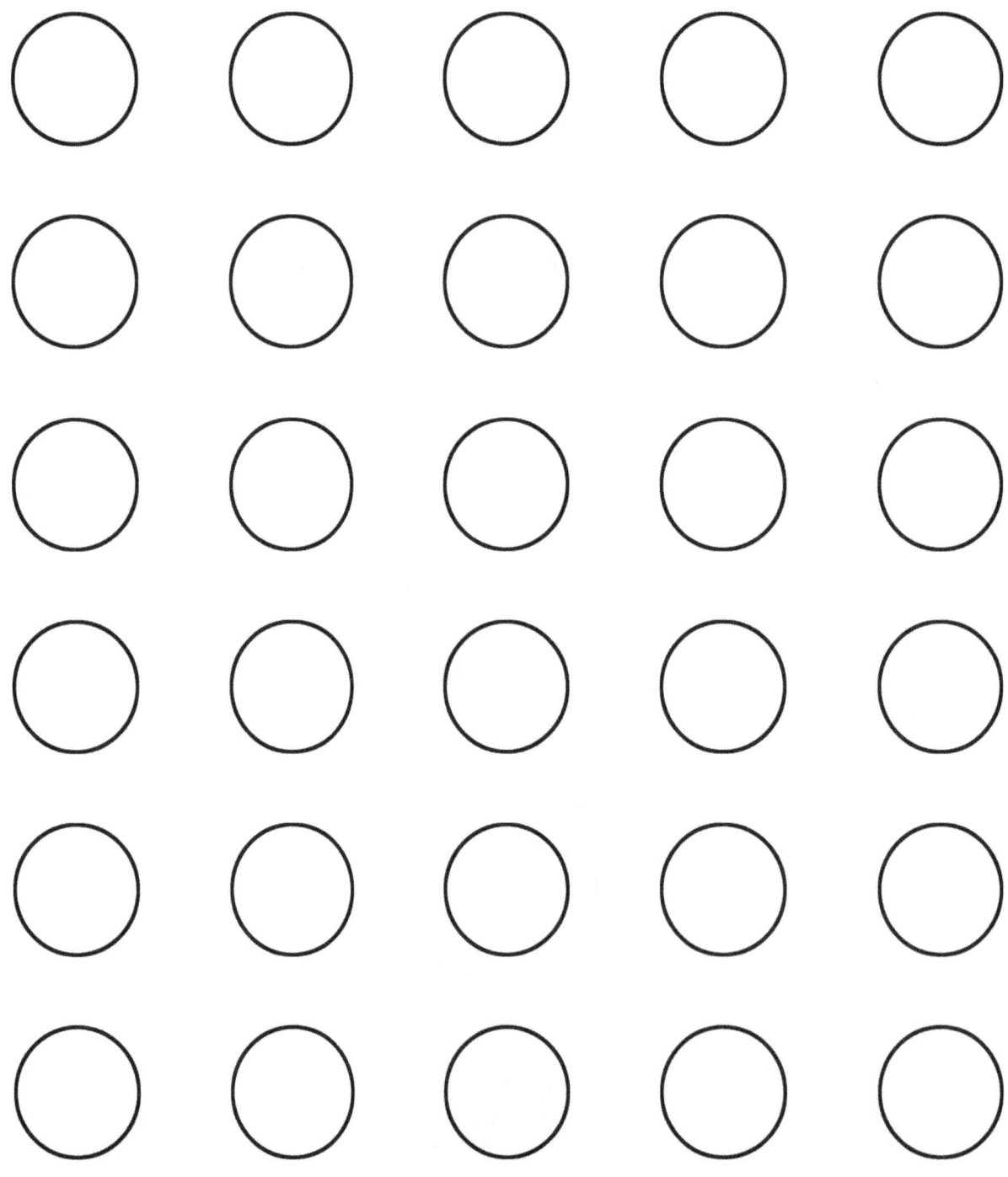

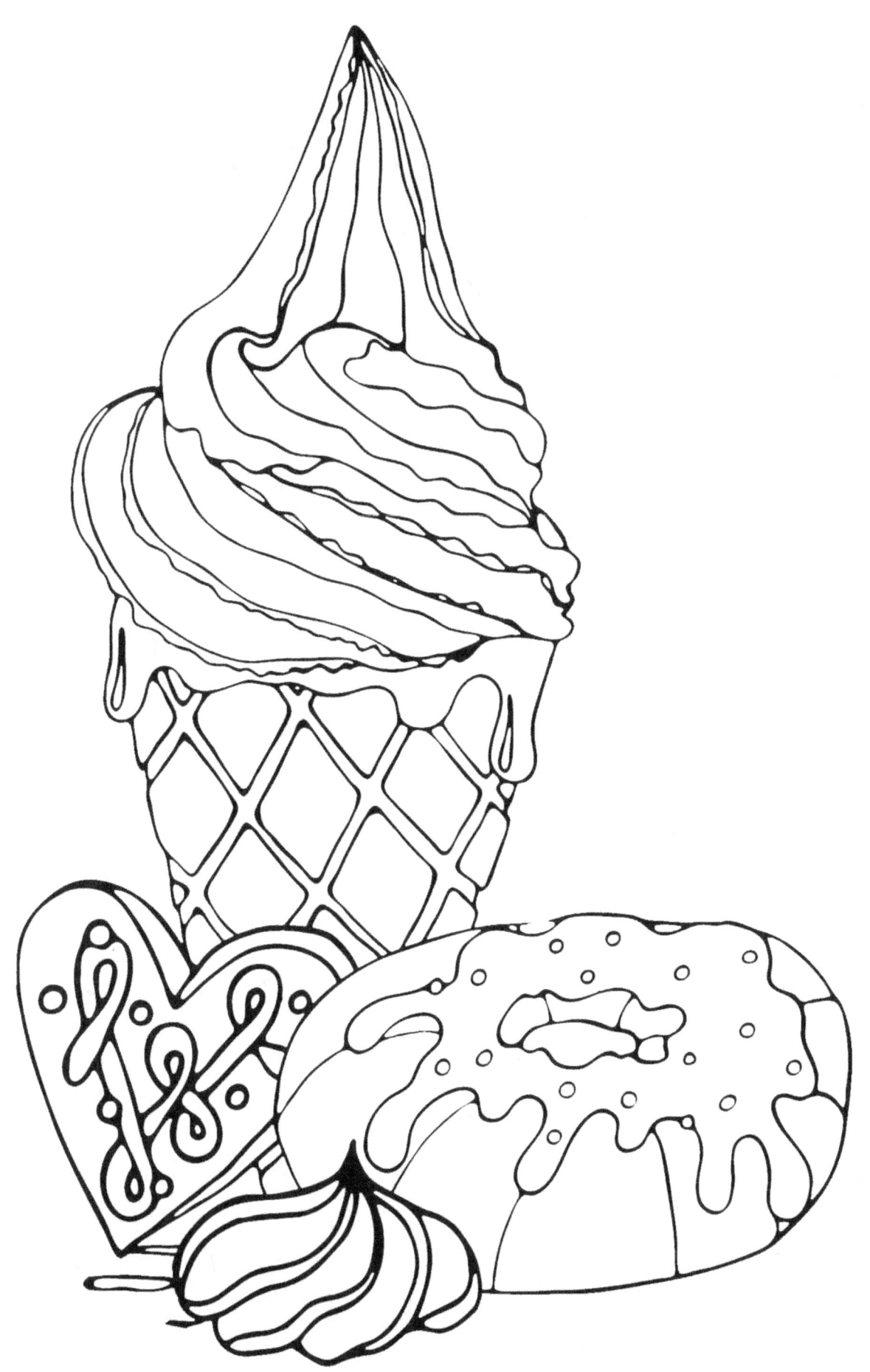

Test Your Color

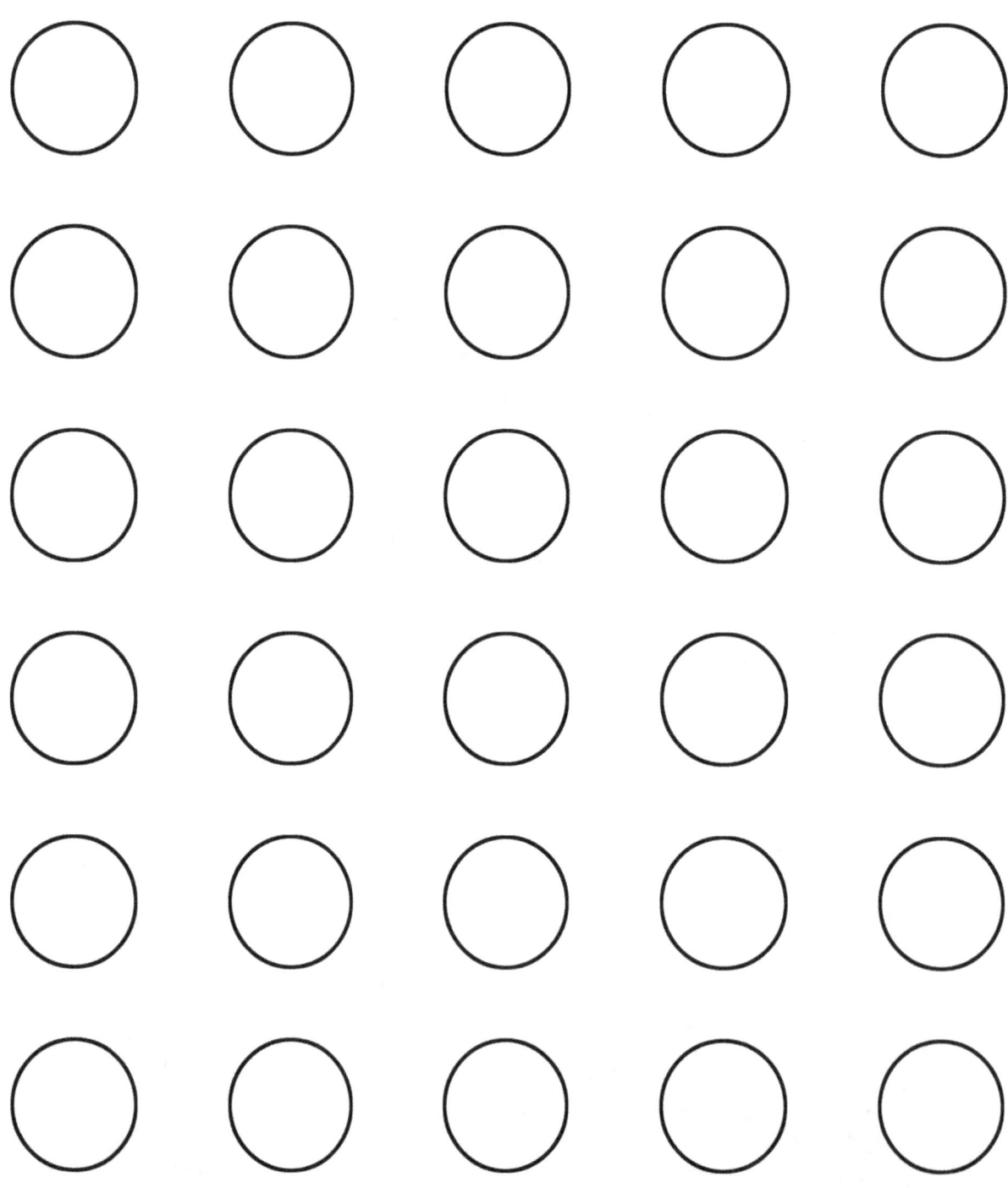

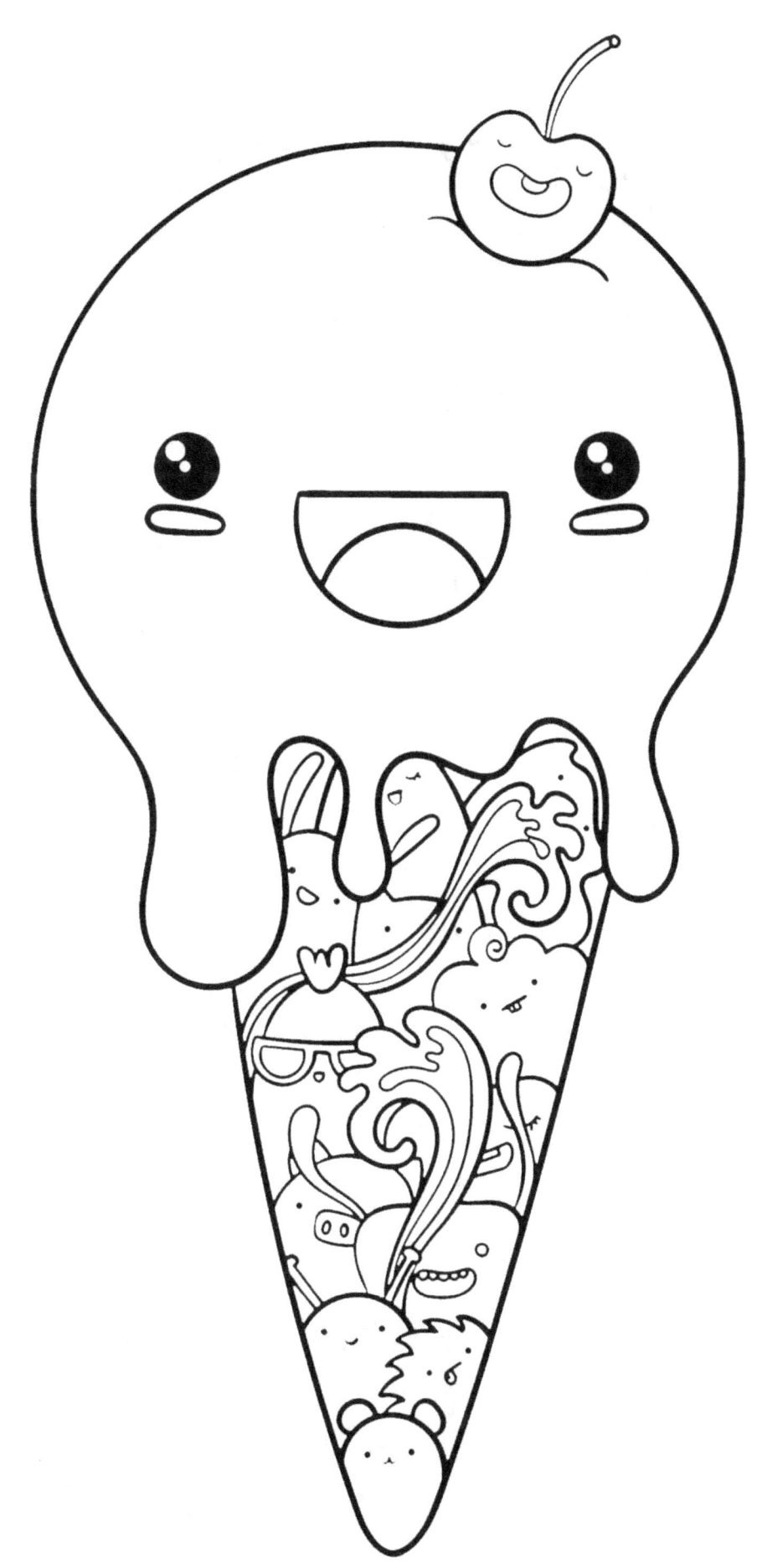

Test Your Color

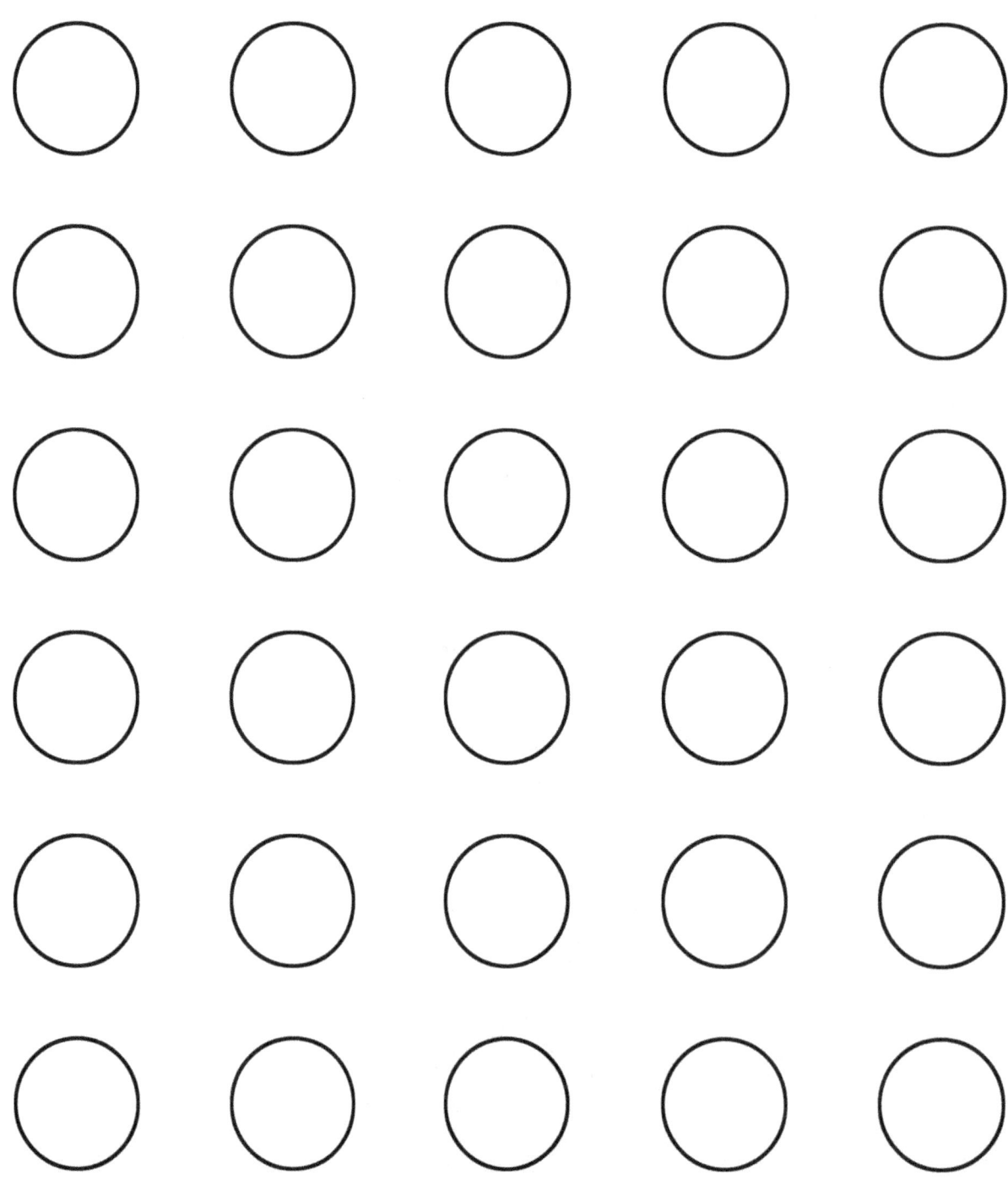

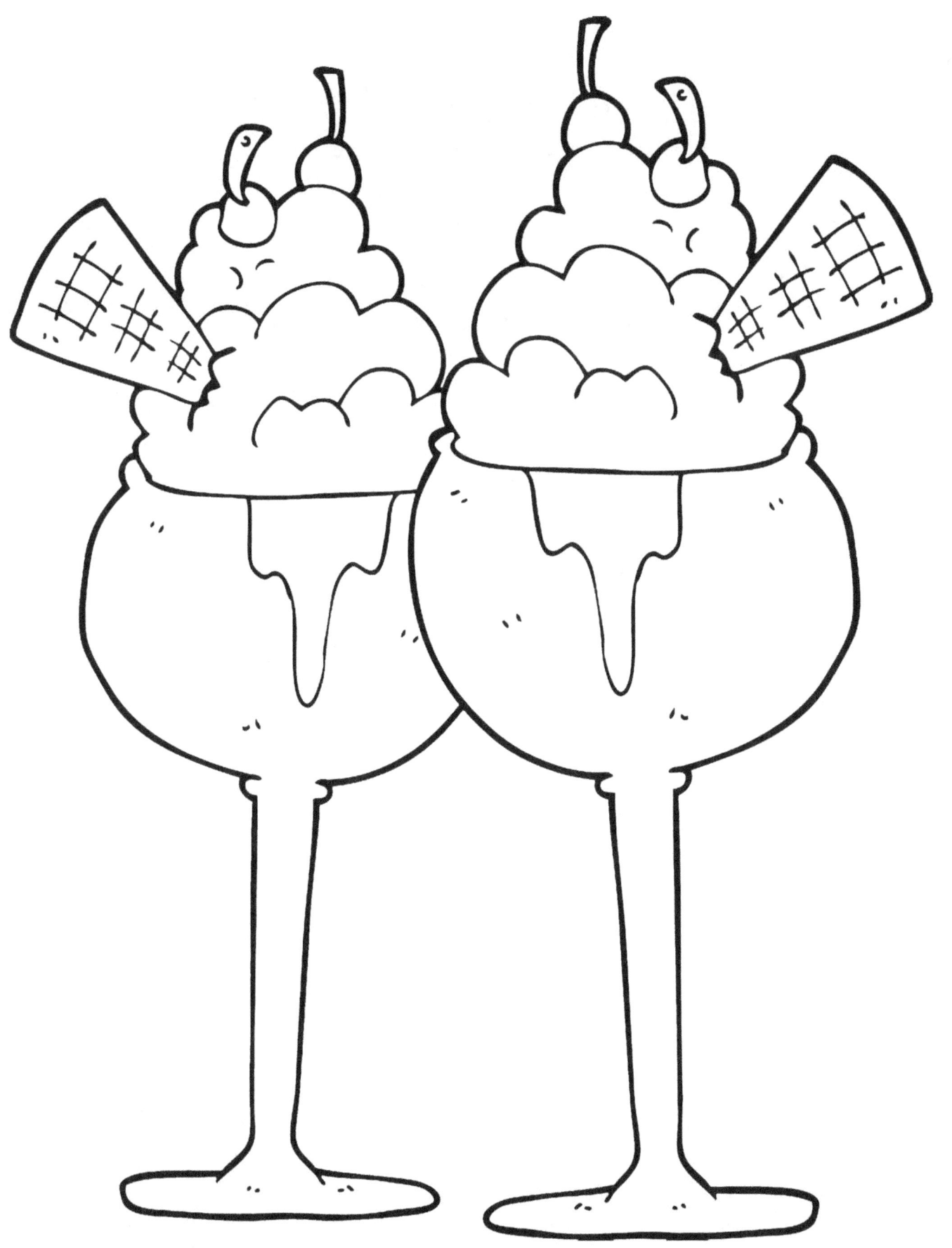

Test Your Color

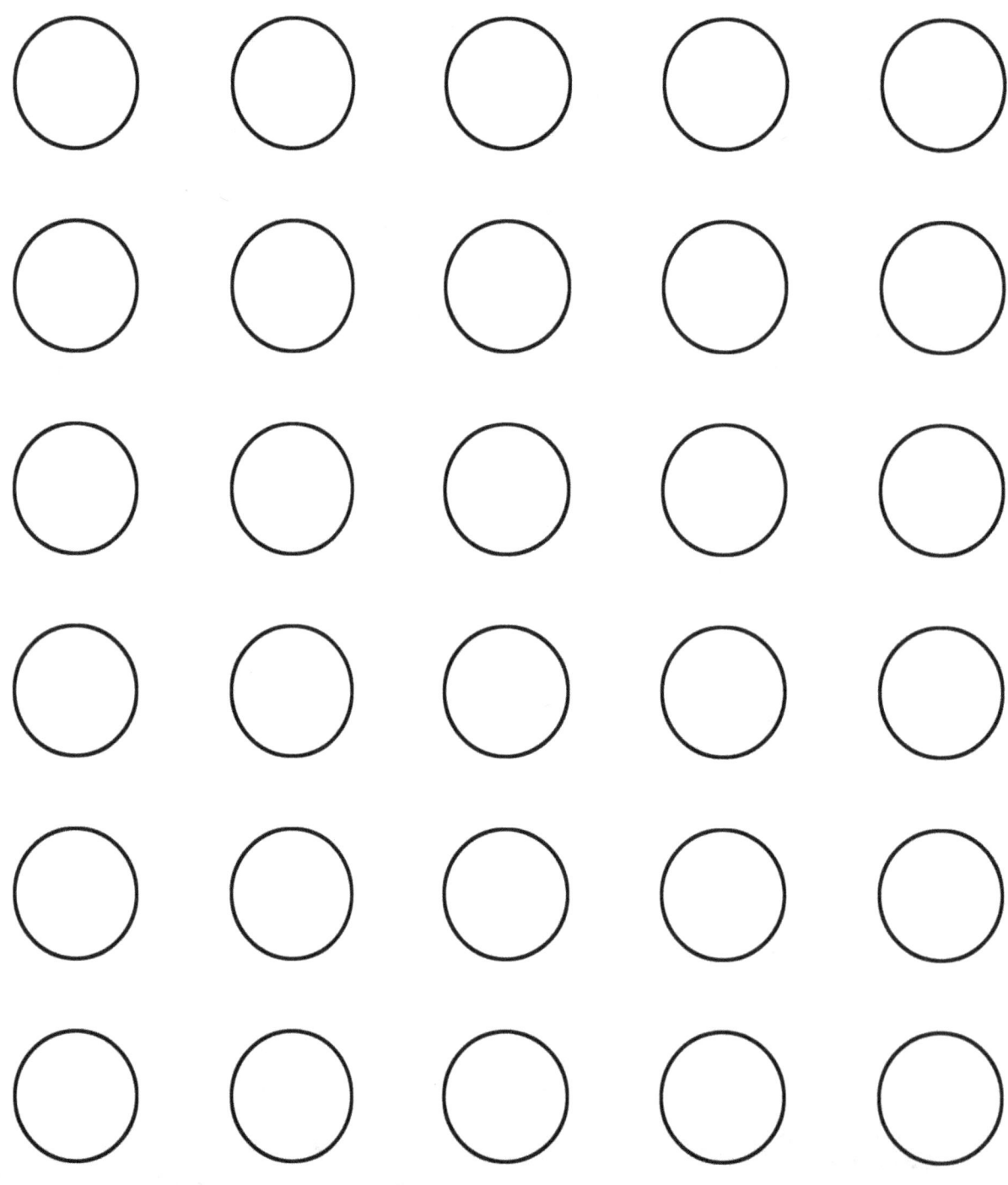

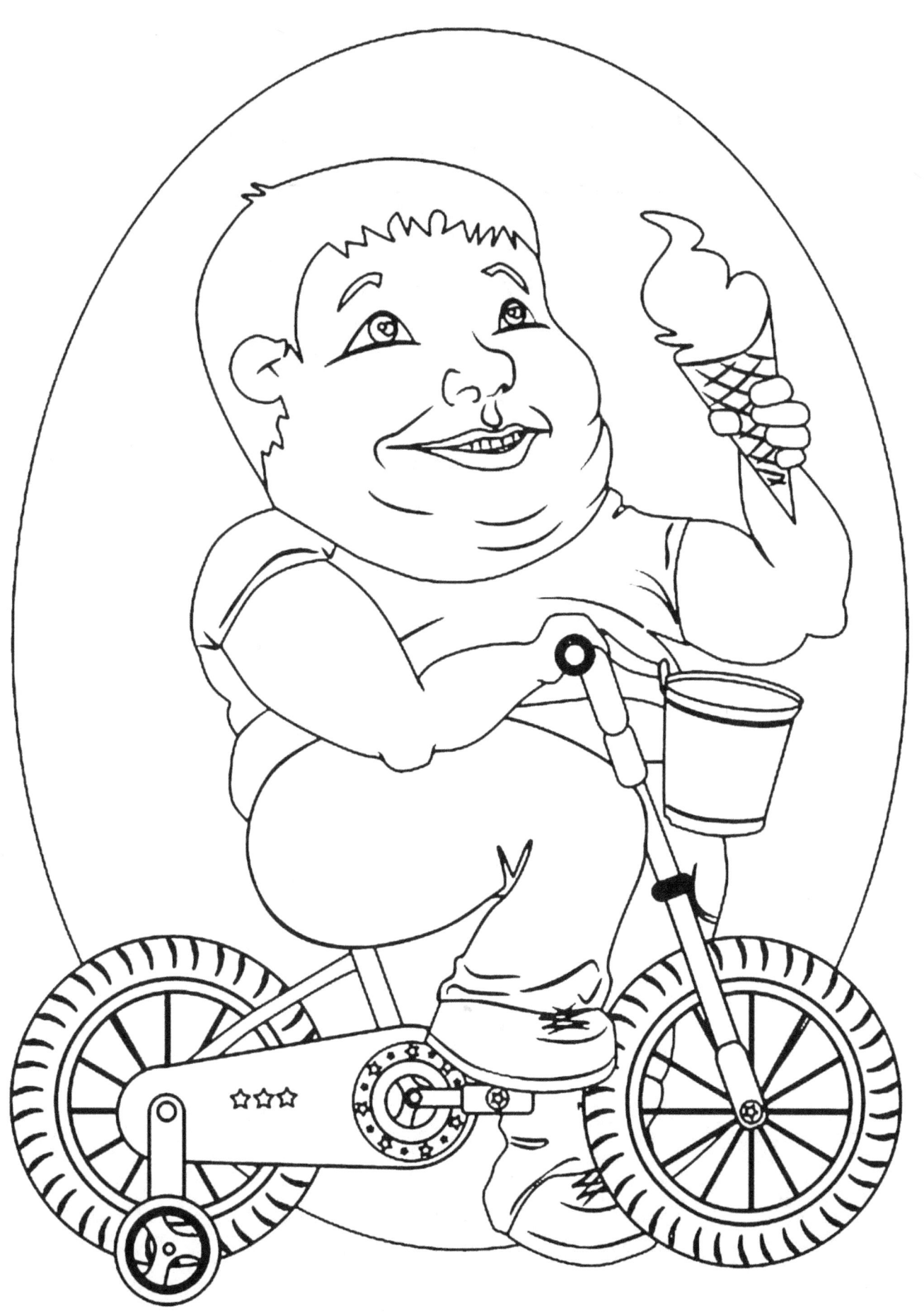

Test Your Color

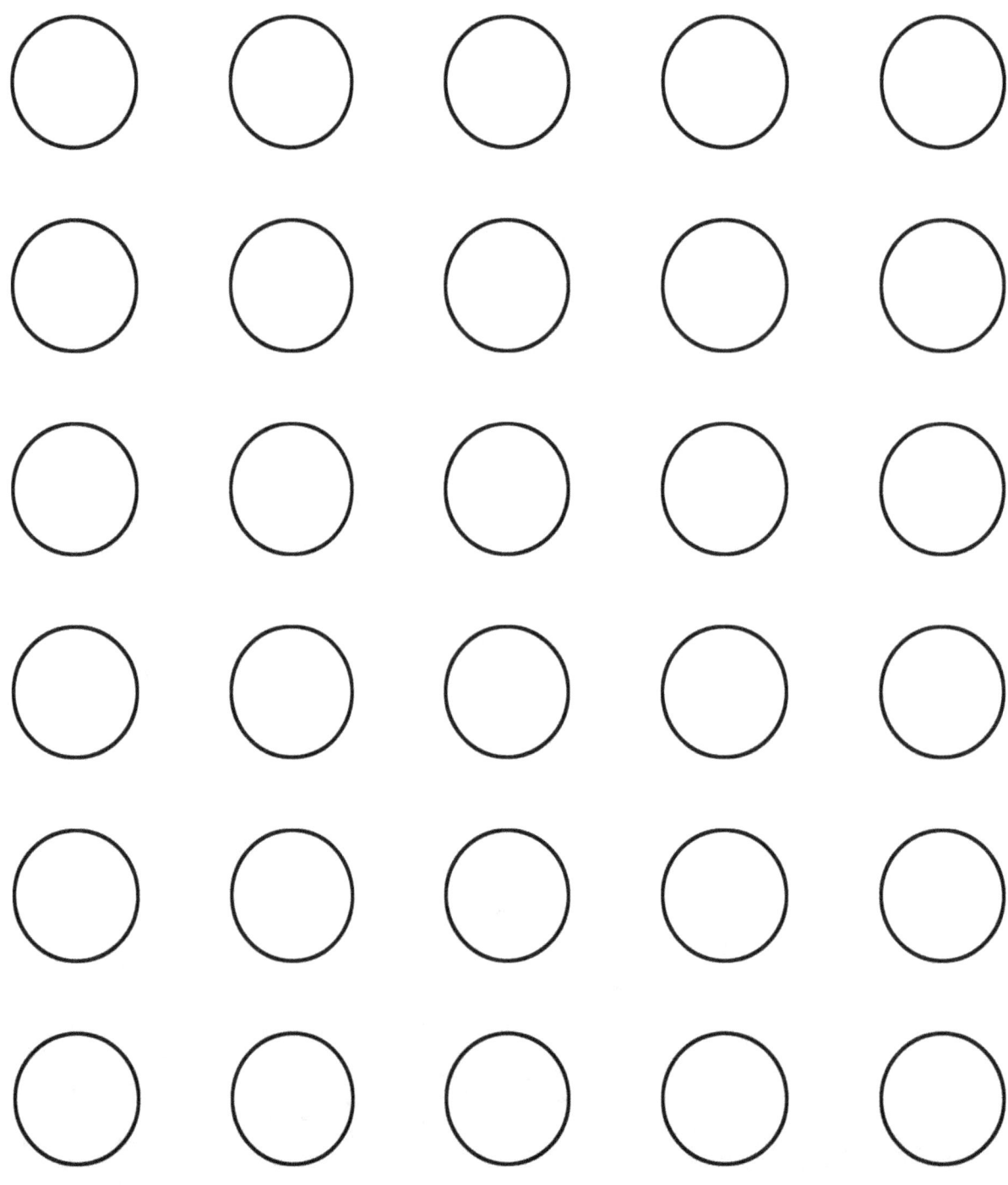

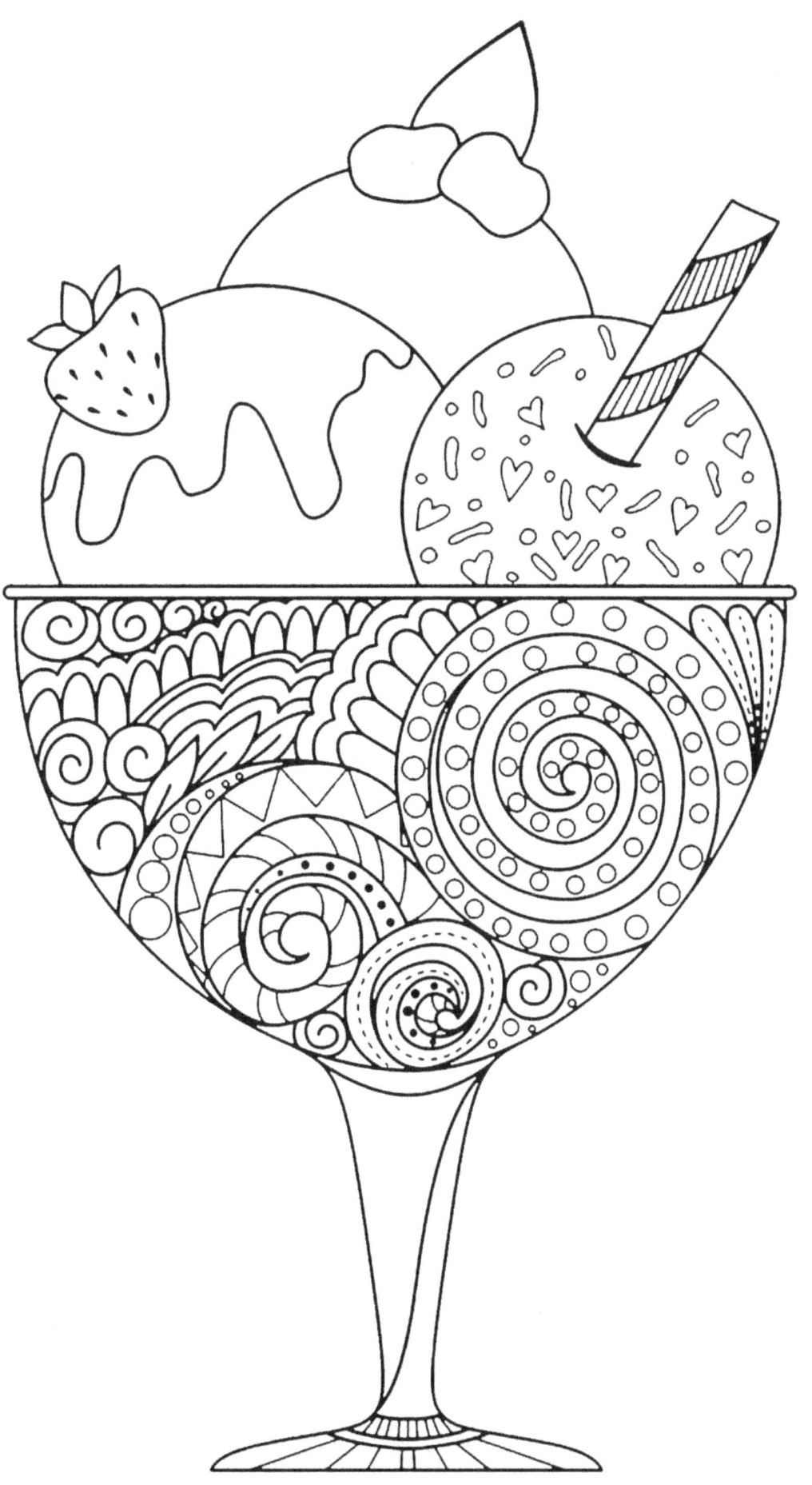

Test Your Color

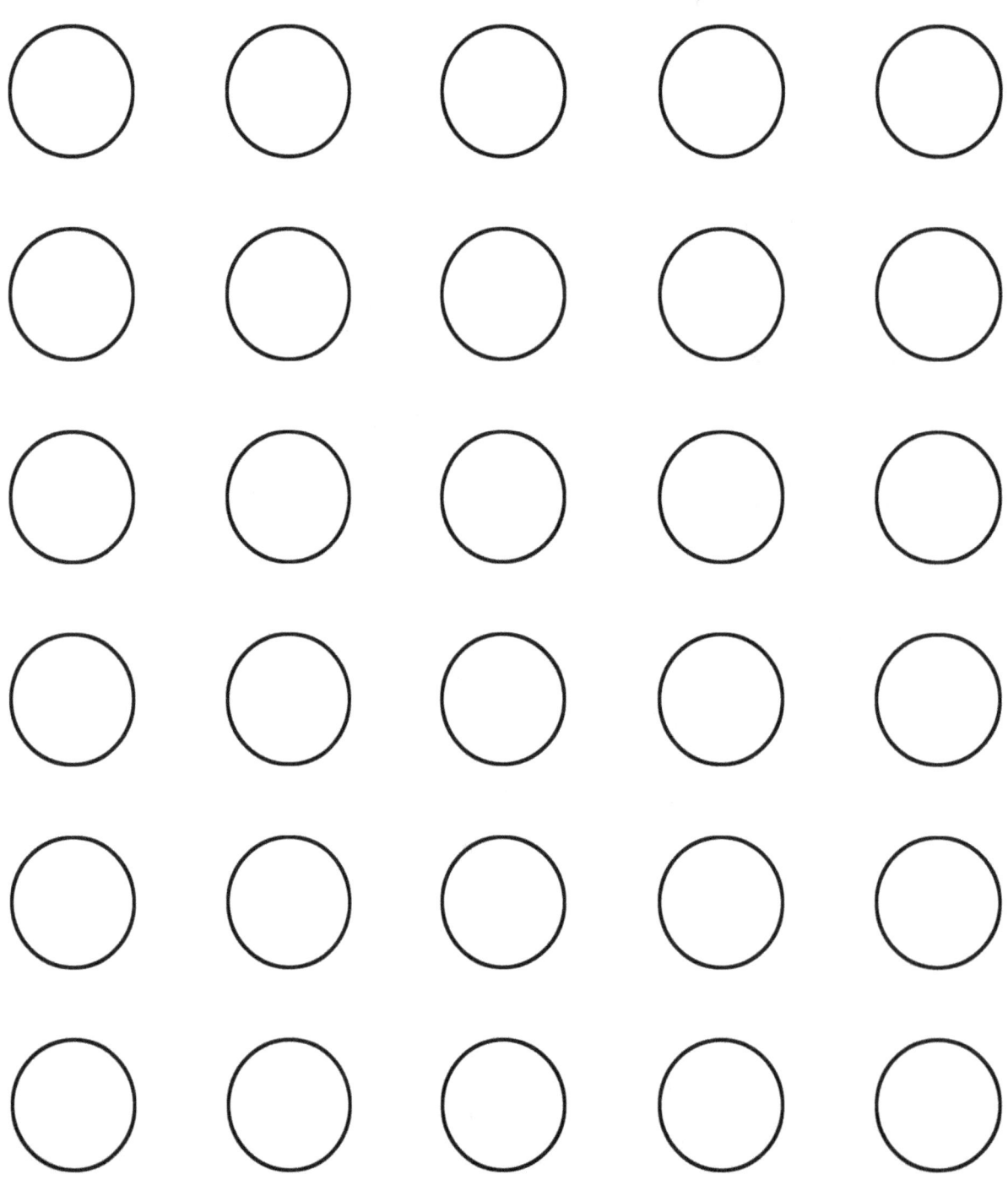

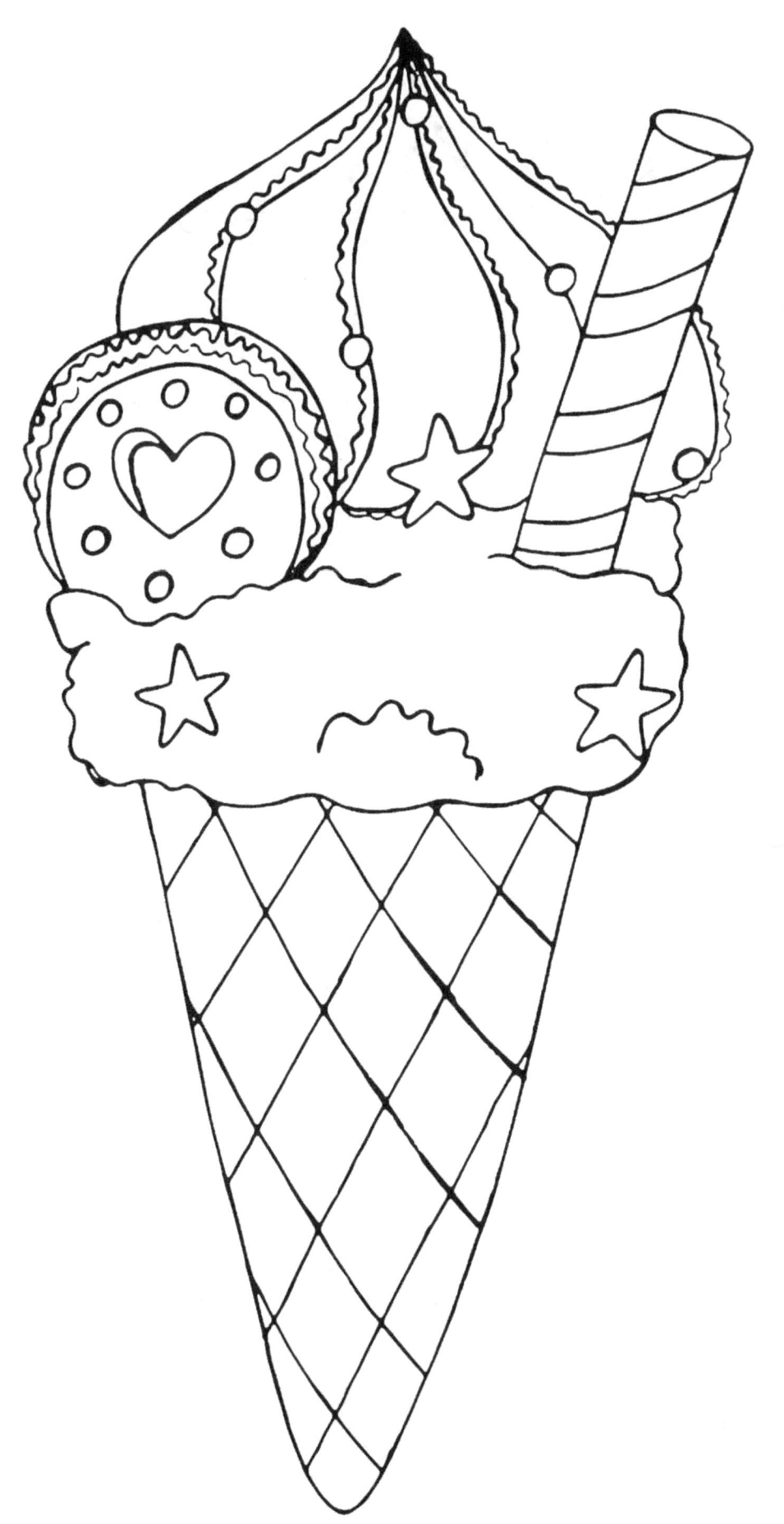

Test Your Color

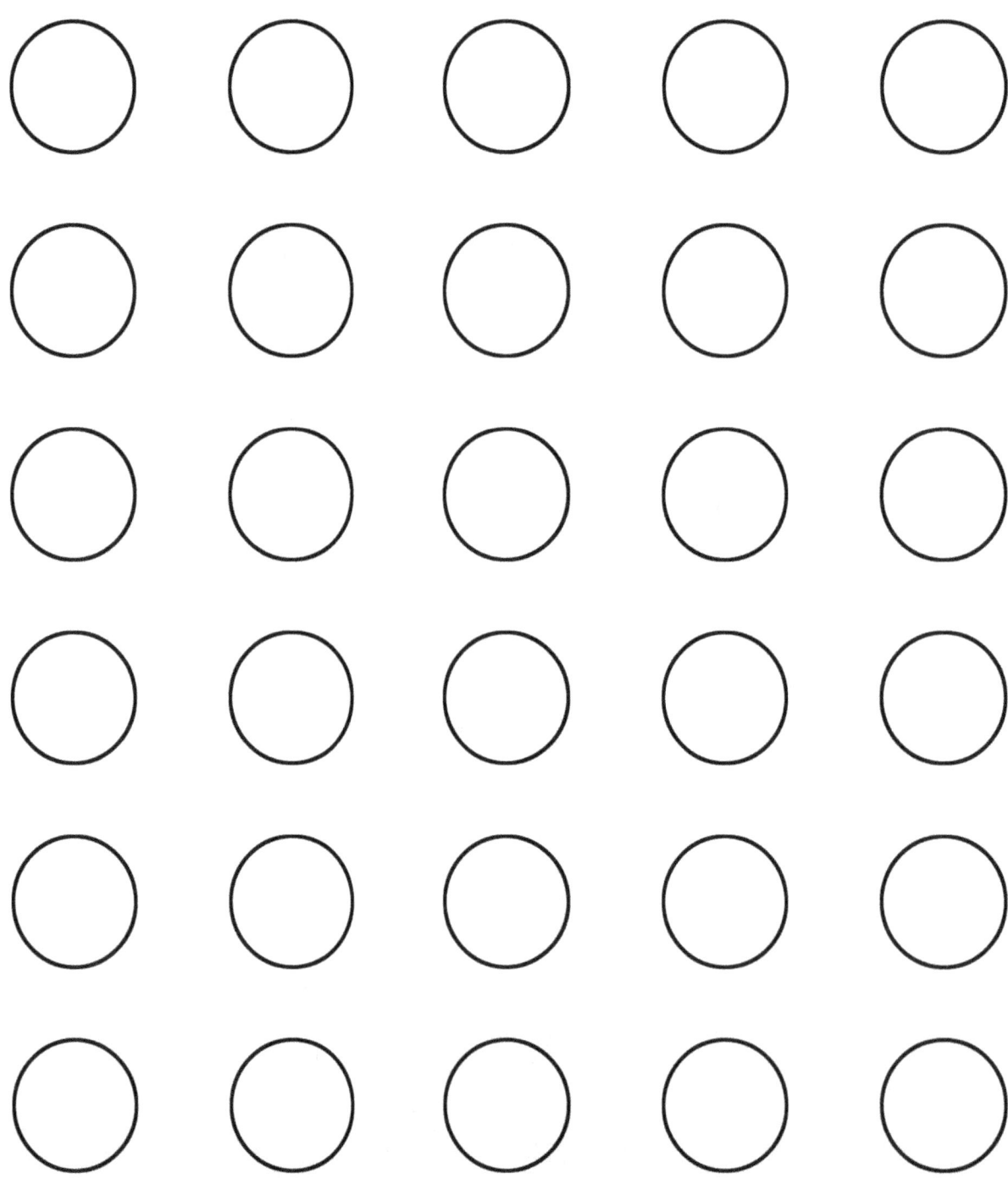

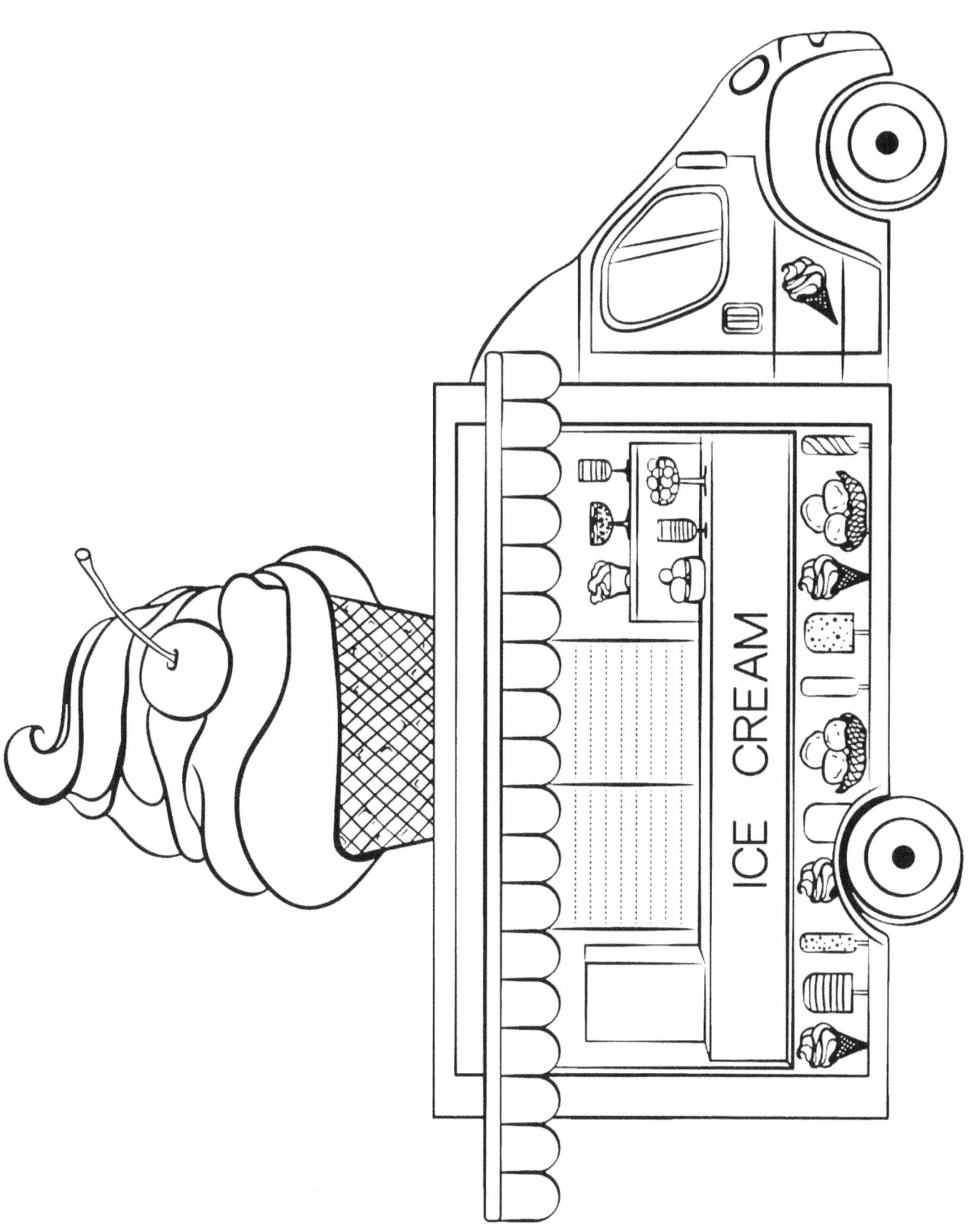

Test Your Color

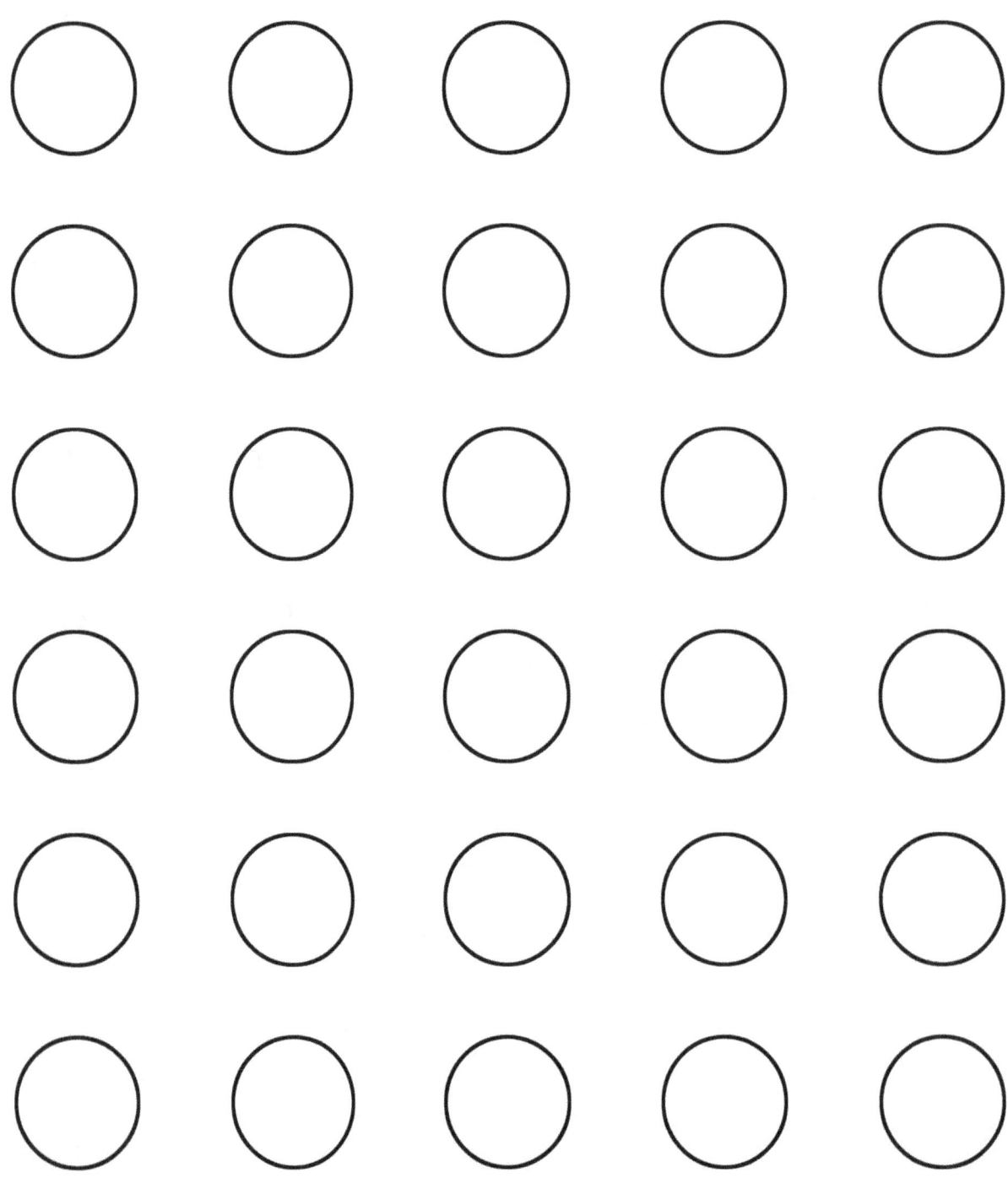

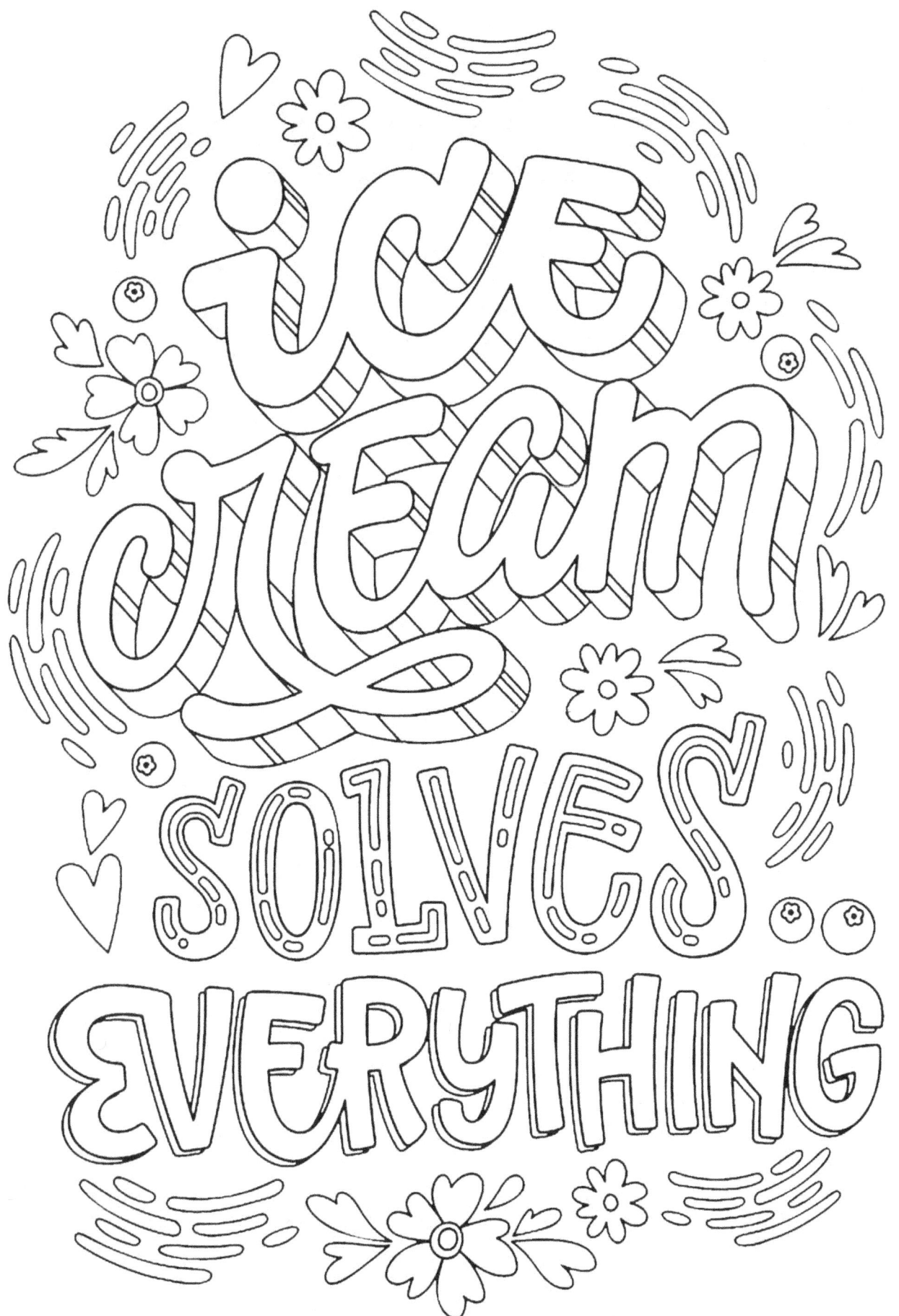

Test Your Color

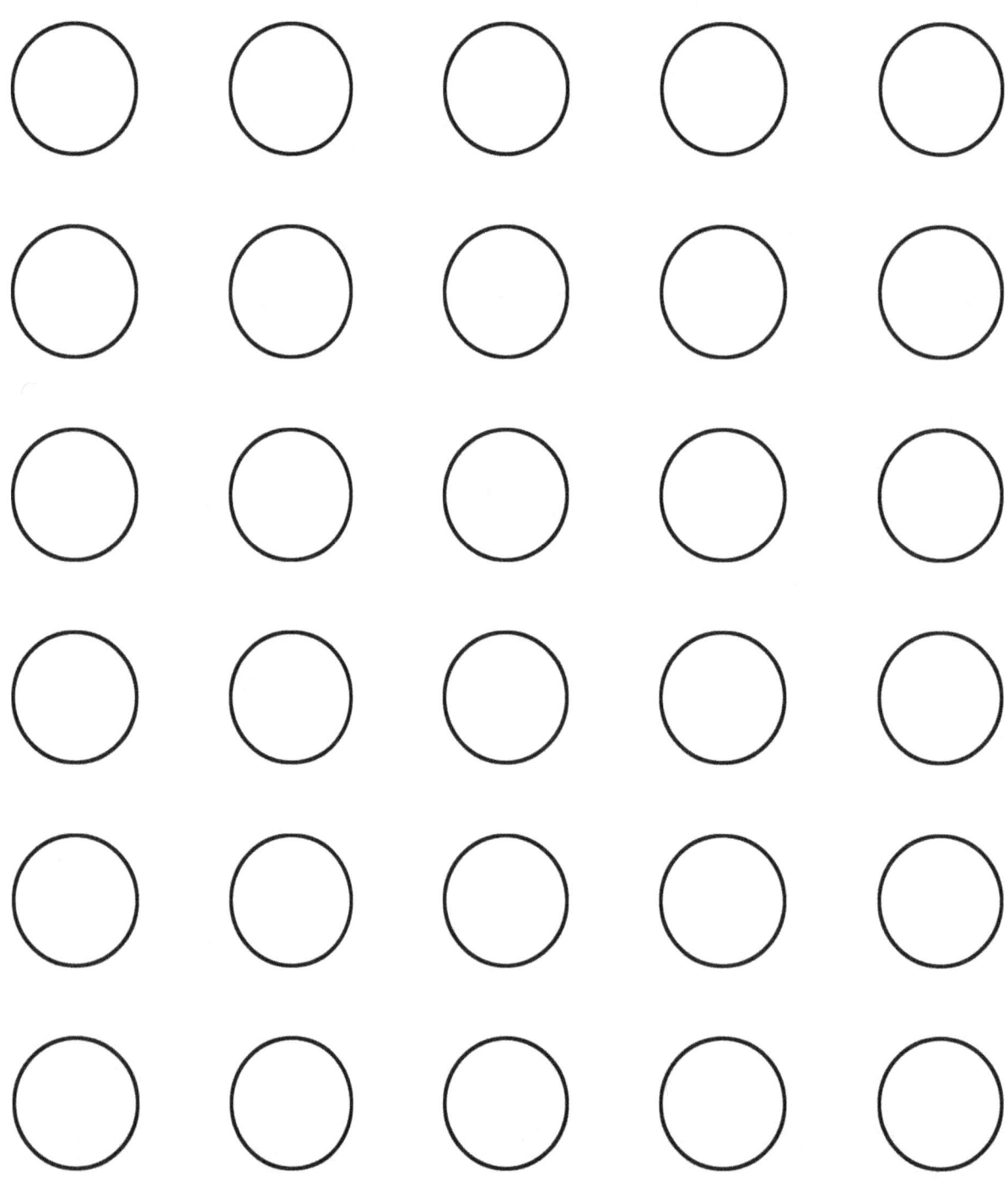

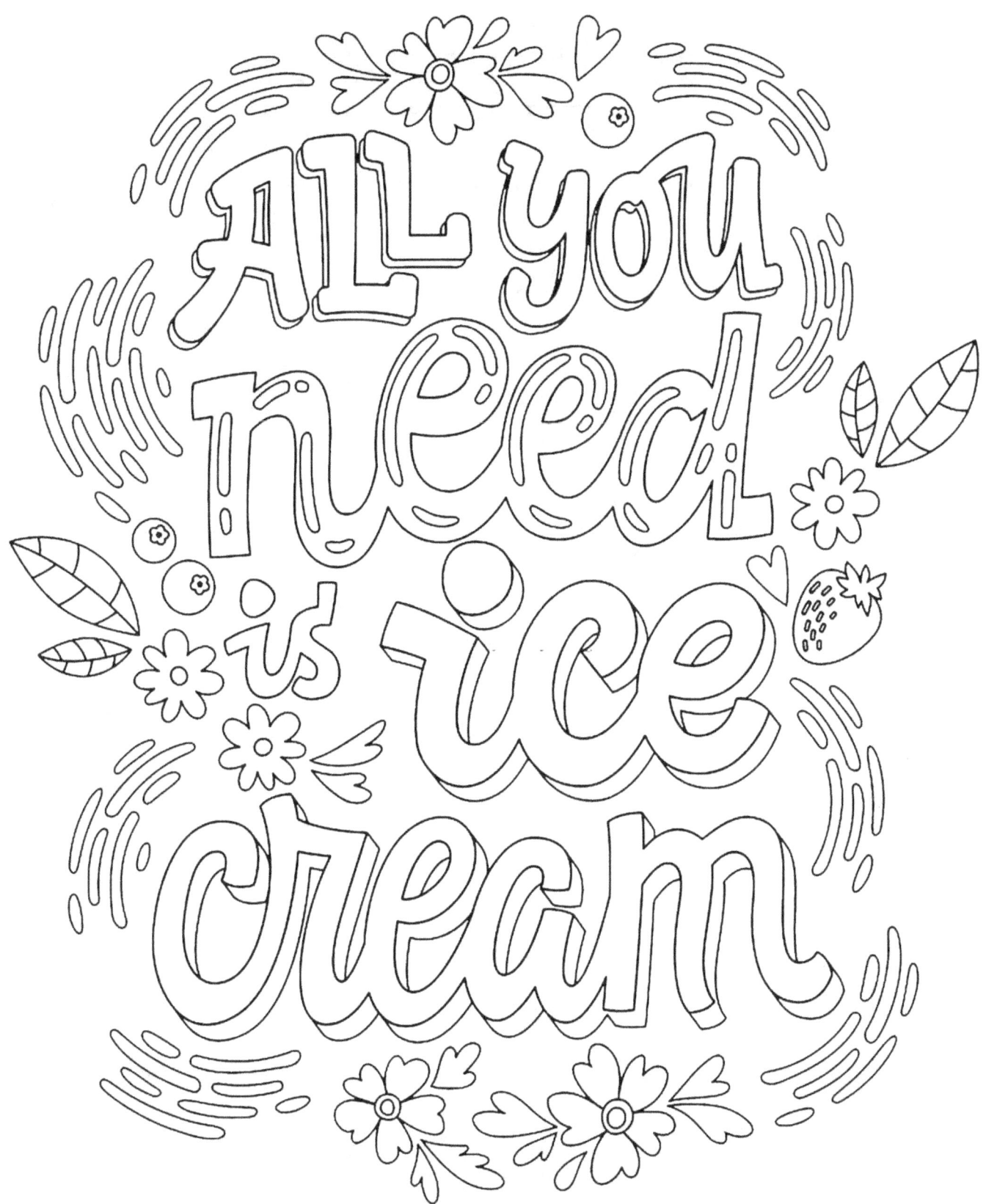

Test Your Color

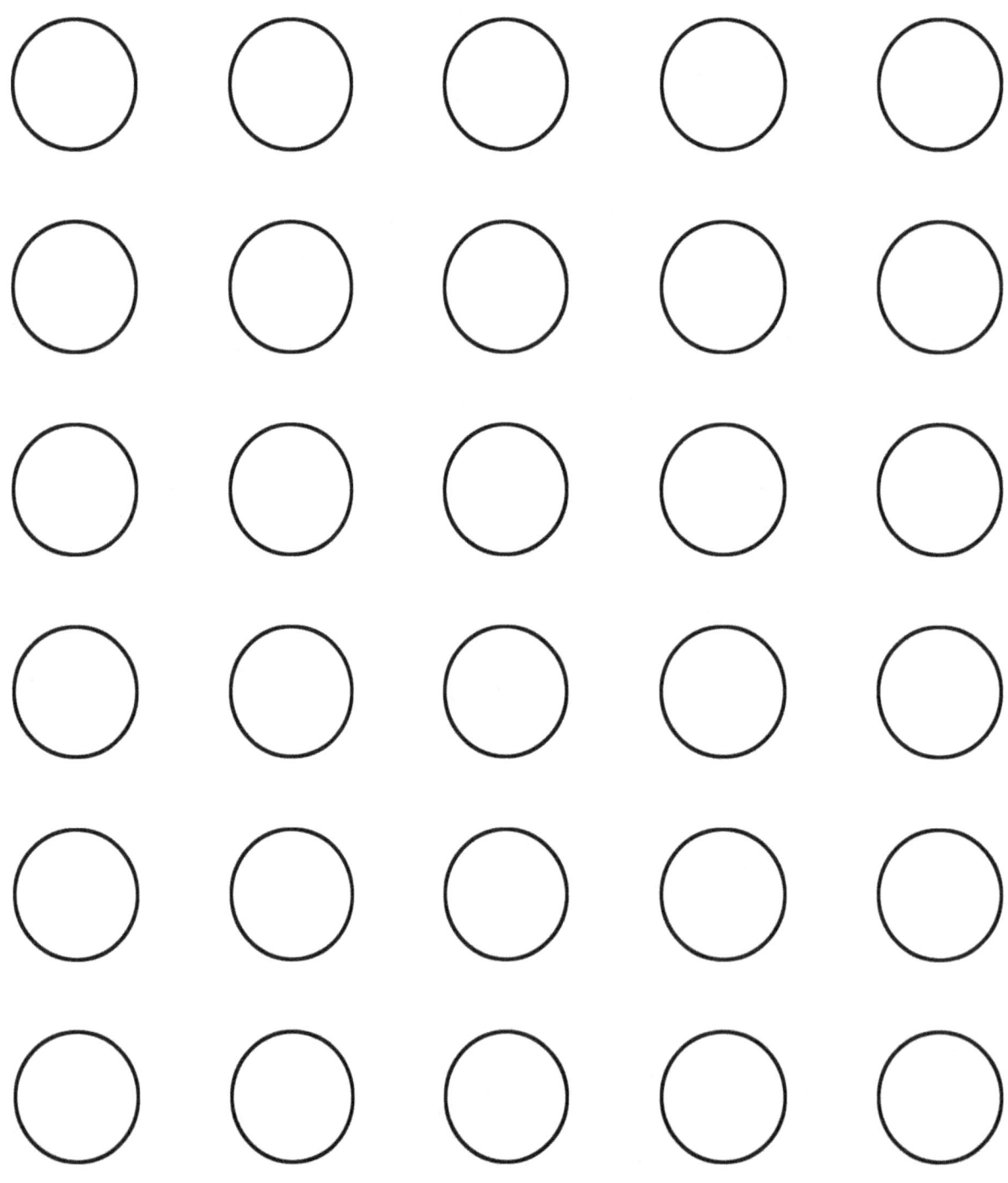